MW00949354

Hey Buddy!

Portraits of Friends

Lawrence F. Lihosit

Cover photo Dra. L.Margarita Solis Kitsu de Lihosit

Printed by KDP, an Amazon.com Company. The printing location may vary, depending upon where the book is to be delivered since this is a Print-On-Demand book.

ISBN 9798850293598

Non-Fiction
Biographies
Peace Corps
Bristol Bay, Alaska
Northeast Bolivia
Honduras
Mexico City
Scottsdale, Arizona

Editor in Chief Will James

Printed in the United States of America

For the next generation

Contents

Introduction

Different friends have always been the secret ingredient. My travels have afforded me many wonderful friends, who when blended with my experiences, made my life richer like hot *atole*. These *vignettes* are word portraits describing some but not all of them.

My middle has widened. I have less teeth and hair. Worse, I now do exercises to keep from tottering. Memories of these friends make me smile. You might enjoy them as well. Be aware that conversations are sometimes vulgar because that's how we yahoos talk. Several of the situations involve deceit, gambling and even unusual sexual practices –*pecados menores*. In other words, these are real people, not living saints. Who would want to stand next to John the Baptist at a wild party? He'd throw a wet blanket on everything! "Repent!"

Some of the situations also involve breaking rules. Before you picture me as a ranting frontiersman waving my rifle in one hand and a flag with a rattlesnake's image in the other, the only time I had my chance at martyrdom I ran as fast as I could. No heroes here. Just an old yahoo thankful for an interesting life surrounded by good friends.

Lawrence F. Lihosit

Hey Buddy!

Fernando Bastida Monterrubio

When we'd finished eating and sat picking our teeth, Fernando mentioned my brother-in-law's car. We were out of there. Downstairs, Fernando ran his index finger along the Mustang's dusty fender, then took a handkerchief from his hip pocket and wiped off the smeared windshield.

"Nice car," he said.

I opened the door. The inside was covered with thick black dust from the smog. Fernando sat down and turned the ignition, cocking his head to one side and listening real close. "It clicks," he said. "Manolo was right: it's probably the starter motor." He climbed out and wiped off his hands, reminding me that before he could work on Manolo's car, he had promised to finish a job on our friend Pancho Ibarra's taxi. They were going to work on it the next day at Petra's house and Fernando told me to come along. Then he looked down for a second. He had noticed that Margarita might not be in a good mood. "Buy her some flowers."

The next morning, I got up before the dogs even howled and walked down to the market. A pretty lady with a gold toothy smile sold me a nice bunch of daisies and gave me change from her large brassiere. The flowers were a tight squeeze into a water jug, but they looked so good that I even sprinkled water on the petals before walking back outside. I flagged down a taxi bound for Santa Anita.

Fernando, Pancho and *Señor* Alfaro, all buddies from the Santa Anita fight, were there. Heck, there were yells and back-slapping hugs all around. Pancho's car hood was up.

"Once we got started, we decided to do an overhaul," explained Fernando.

Pancho climbed under the car. I rolled up my sleeves while Fernando searched for an extra pair of overalls. They made me the honorary go-fer. Fernando crawled under to disconnect the transmission while Pancho worked the engine mounts. *Señor* Alfaro worked a pulley. I grabbed screwdrivers and wrenches on command. We had the engine

11

out. It was broken down piece by piece, Fernando inspecting each part while the others watched and listened.

"How long has it been since anyone looked at this alternator?" Fernando asked Pancho.

"It was rebuilt two months ago."

"You had them repack it with used ball bearings! You cheap *burro*. They have to be replaced again." Pancho blushed and *Señor* Alfaro laughed, then Pancho. "Don't worry," said Fernando, "We can fix anything. The impossible just takes longer."

Señor Alfaro took something else apart. A bolt snapped and he swore. Fernando looked over, then stood, dusting off his overalls. Back in his shed we heard a clatter. Returning he spilled a coffee can full of spare bolts on the concrete. *Señor* Alfaro picked one up and nodded.

We worked until dusk when Petra called out that the food was ready. We carefully covered the engine and parts with an old tarp. The screws and bolts were laid in neat rows. *Señor* Alfaro swept. Pancho covered the front of his car with a cloth. I washed down the driveway with a hose. We wiped our hands and arms with gasoline, then soap and water before sitting down at the simple table set with bowls of beans, *tortillas* and slices of cactus which had been cooked with onions and spices.

Señor Alfaro, a man with giant arms, served himself some beans with a wooden spoon that tapped the bowl as he dug in. "Lorenzo. Last week my son's taxi got stolen."

"Carlos?" asked Pancho.

Señor Alfaro nodded as he spooned *chiles* onto his plate. "You know where it was stolen? At a downtown theater. He went to see a movie with his wife and family."

Fernando shook his head and took a hot *tortilla* from the basket, flipping it from hand to hand for a second. *Señor* Alfaro used a piece of his *tortilla* like a spoon for his beans. "So we go to the police station to file a report. They ask for rewards and we say sure. Next day they call us. 'We found the car,' they say. There it was in the police yard, stripped of radio and tires. We had to pay the police for a reward and then fix the car. That was three months wages." He let his *tortilla* drop onto his plate. "Damn! They're the ones who stole it."

Petra filled our glasses with juice of *jamaica* mixed with water. It was red and sweet. My glass formed beads of sweat that ran down onto the plastic covered table

"The police are worse than before," said Pancho and bit into his rolled up *tortilla* filled with beans. "Fernando. When will my car be back on the road?"

"Tomorrow, we take the valves and drive shaft to the machine shop and drop them off. You take those ball bearings down the street for replacement today. We can spray paint the hood area too."

"Blue. I want blue."

"Blue? The car is orange. It will look like a Mexican mural when you open the hood."

"I already bought the paint. It's for Indians anyway."

It took longer. Three days later, Petra's gate clanked shut behind me just after they had lowered the engine back into place. The inside hood area was painted an aquamarine blue. So was the engine block.

"Look at that engine!" said Fernando. "I had some black paint. He wouldn't use it."

"I had the blue paint left over from painting my son's bicycle."

The remount began as a quick project, with drive train and clutch all meshed and set. The carburetor was fitted and bolted on, the hoses, the radiator and fan, the belts returned and adjusted. Everything was tightened and inspected. Fernando had me crawl underneath. He held a flashlight, pointing to one of the motor mounts.

"That was so oxidized that it was ready to cave in. We welded on a new piece and look at this!" We crawled out. He pointed to other places where they had cut away rusted portions of car body and welded on patches so well that I had to run my hand across to feel them.

Señor Alfaro pulled a bottle of *tequila* from a bag. Fernando got some glasses with ice and cola from the house.

We toasted Pancho's blue engine. Fernando shook his head and said, "Blue."

"It's for Indians anyway," said Pancho as we clinked glasses.

Days passed. Communion at Fernando's mother's Mass was a must but a Confession was necessary first. Us Catholics are like that, what the hey. A priest gave regular Confessions near my mother-in-law's house so I tiptoed down because I hadn't been picking grapes for the Lord's vineyard. Lucky for me there wasn't much of a line and I quietly slipped into a dark Confessional. On the other side of a wooden panel, a priest slid open his shaded port hole. I could see his shadow making the Sign of the Cross. I cleared my throat and began in Spanish. My part took the longest, most naturally.

He made the magical signs and said, "Five Our Fathers...and...are you a foreigner?"

I told him that I was his northern neighbor. "Three Rosaries," he said and slid his porthole shut.

That's a lot of praying by golly but it was worth it because Romualda had been a special friend. From the very first meetings in Santa Anita, she had the sort of confidence that was catchy like a good fast tune. No matter what happened, it was her jokes that made us smile and her food that kept us fit. When things got really dangerous, just before the men with guns came looking for me, Romualda appeared to me in a dream and warned me. That's when I went underground and finally, left the country.

At least part of a Mass like this is remembering and that's exactly what I was doing as Margarita and I walked around the corner from Chabacano metro station to Santa Teresa Church. It was really a *capilla* nestled between two tall apartment buildings. The narrow church was under the apartment's shadows because the sun was just rising and the dew was still frozen on the sidewalk. Our steps left white footprints. During the Mass, the light of a new day filtered red, blue, orange and yellow through the dozens of small arched stained-glass windows.

Afterwards, while we stood on the damp sidewalk under sunlight, trying to talk over the din of morning traffic, Fernando's sister invited us over to her house for a breakfast. She served us all hot *atole,* a thick sweet corn drink and corn *tamales* filled with shredded beef and *chiles:* our Mexican Communion. There was plenty of time to shake hands with all her children who had grown so tall. Mostly though, there were stories about Romualda. At the age of fourteen, her father explained to her that with so many children, he couldn't afford to feed her anymore. She went to Mexico City and worked for the next fourteen years as a house maid. During that time, she bought a lot in the northern part of the city by paying a weekly installment. Not long after completing payment, she married. Soon, her father died and there was legal work to be prepared. Romualda's father had the right to a piece of community property in Santa Anita. She and her husband got to work. After months, a legal deed was brought forward for her signature. That's when her husband found out that she was illiterate. So, he taught his twenty-eight-year-old bride to read with the newspaper. Until the day that she died, almost a half century later, Romualda read the newspaper each day.

We set our empty glasses down. "We should go visit Chucho, He's in jail. You know how he gets when he drinks."

"When?"

"Tomorrow if you want."

"We should stop in the market and buy food and cigarettes."

"Chucho doesn't smoke."

"He can barter with them. Remember, we can't take much money or the guards will get it. Oh, you'll need some identification."

Identification? Identify myself after the warnings? Who knows if men in fancy suits with holstered pistols in the middle of their back were still looking for me? Heck, my plan was to fib. I'd been saving up sins for a really good Confession and figured one more fib would fit into the deck like a wild card. Fernando asked me if I still had my Mexican driver's license. Holding the receiver between my ear and shoulder, I tried to reach into my denim pocket, but after all them *tacos al pastor,* my pants had shrunk. So, I stood up and pulled out the black, creased wallet and rummaged through the back sections. Sure enough, I found the Mexican driver's license that didn't even mention my nationality. Years ago, a Junior Club friend who happened to be in charge of a police station fixed me up. It was out of date, but it had a picture on it. Fernando told me to leave all other identification at home, just in case.

"If anyone is looking for you," he said, "They're looking for a *gringo,* not a Mexican. Just let me talk. You've got an accent."

Not talk? My father was a salesman! Not only that, but my wife always told me that my accent in Spanish was cute. You kin be wrong.

My mother-in-law jumped and shouted the next morning as she walked into the kitchen and found me sitting at the table all alone, drinking fresh brewed coffee. Once she pulled her robe closed tight to the neck, resettled her glasses straight on her face, she broke eggs for everyone's breakfast.

"Oriental?" she asked. I nodded. "Send my regards to Chucho. Tell him that he is in my prayers."

The downstairs gate buzzer sounded. I opened the window. Below, on the street, stood Fernando alongside his taxi, waving. We were off.

We drove down Ermita Ixtapalapa past the Cerro de las Estrellas and into the commercial district of Ixtapalapa. What a name. It took me quite a spell to pronounce it and even longer to learn how to spell it. Mexico City is divided into districts like New York's boroughs. Each district has a major government plaza with courts, administrative offices, police stations and a commercial zone complete with a public market.

Fernando backed into a parking space across the street from the market entrance. It was made of poured concrete, with concrete floors and a corrugated metal roof,

16

creating echoes. Near the triple wide entrance, there were rows of fresh flowers, petals glistening from water that the vendors sprinkled on them. The air was filled with many smells: flowers, oil, coal dust, freshly chopped kindling, cooking beef, minced onions and fish. There were piles of cantaloupes, some sliced in half. A woman handed me a slice of pink watermelon that dripped over my hand. There was a hardware section where a man wearing a white apron scooped out gobs of wax onto newsprint that lay atop an old scale.

We bought a couple of clear plastic bags for easy inspection at the prison. Fernando threw in a couple of cantaloupes, then convinced the woman I bartered with to lower the price of a very small watermelon by thirty percent. As we walked down to the vegetables, he shook his head, muttered, "Accent..." Within twenty minutes, we carried four large bags filled with onions, carrots, potatoes, cantaloupe, watermelon, oranges, grapefruit, pineapples, tortillas, cheese and even some bread. Finally, we bought twenty packs of different brands of cigarettes.

The sun rose above roofs. The sunlight glinted on Fernando's taxi's windshield. Inside, speckles of dust danced in the air, illuminated like fireflies as we took out our pocketknives, then most of our money.

We hid them under the plastic floor mats that were now warm to the touch. We both kept a bit of money in secret hiding places, just in case. The twenty packs of cigarettes were strewn across his seat and we both fidgeted as we slid a pack here and a pack there inside our clothes. Cigarettes were contraband.

The Oriental prison was very close to the market. Since the city had grown so fast, its high cement wall with gun towers overlooked homes and streets. There were uniformed men carrying automatic rifles on each corner and even across the street inside of a tiny store where Fernando and me drank a warm cola while staring straight ahead, silently.

We walked across to the main entrance to the prison. A fat man in a rumpled green uniform sat on a folding chair just inside the door. He asked for identification. We were ready. He glanced at our cards and handed us each a colored piece of paper.

"Lose this and you don't get out."

Fernando nodded coolly, walked inside the huge building with a forty-foot high, beamed ceiling. Crowds talked to guards. Voices echoed. Fernando pointed off to a lady who stood inside a glassed-in booth.

There were others asking about cellblocks and directions so we waited our turn. Fernando waited patiently and addressed her as *señorita* as she thumbed through a stack of three by five cards. After a few minutes, Fernando placed a folded bill on the counter. She scooped it up and asked which prisoner we wanted to know about. Fernando told her and she thumbed through cards.

"He's not listed," she said and then checked another name for someone else, ignoring us.

Fernando looked over his shoulder at me and waved for me to move back. When she returned to the counter, he handed her another folded bill and asked that she look again. There was another stack of three by five cards and she pulled one with frayed, brown edges.

"It's not his visiting day unless you're his lawyer."

Fernando waved me back farther. He talked to the young woman softly and she pointed to a desk on the other side of the building. Fernando straightened up, walked towards the desk, stopping just long enough to wave me back even farther until I stood near the door, next to the man in the green rumpled uniform. I watched Fernando shake hands with another man in regular street clothes. Fernando moved his hands around in the air and nodded his head. The man he talked to was silent until the last, when he shook his head and turned. Fernando followed him, moving his hands more frantically and stooping his shoulders as one hand slipped into his own pants pocket very quickly, then came out and shook hands with the man. Fernando pointed at me and talked some more. There was one more handshake before Fernando waved me over.

The man in regular clothes wore a black plastic nameplate that read **Bravo**. "It's a pleasure to meet you *Licenciado,*" he said to me and shook my hand. "Even lawyers must present identification, please." An over polite man is hidin' some mighty unpolite thoughts.

I handed him my Mexican driver's license that did not mention my nationality without opening my big mouth, like Fernando had suggested. Bravo studied the license, then handed it back. "An unfortunate oversight, *Licenciado*. This license expired last year. Do you have any other identification?"

While Fernando distracted him with small talk about birthdays and how easy it is to forget to update a driver's license, I reached into my pocket and palmed a folded bill, then shook hands with Bravo. As he felt the bill against his palm, he nodded, then reached for his desk. Grabbing a pencil and paper, he wrote a short note, to explain that my license was enough. He handed me the note, pointed to a turnstile and dressing rooms. We had to be frisked. Fernando and I were separated and led away.

A uniformed guard entered the tiny changing room with me. "Please empty all of your pockets on this bench, *Licenciado.*" I placed some money and keys on an unvarnished wooden bench. "Is that all, *Licenciado?*" I nodded. "Fine. Please lean against the wall with your hands higher than your head. Spread your legs farther apart than your shoulders."

First he noticed that my love handles were square. "Could you please remove these and put them on the bench?"

Next he noticed that my testicles were square also. I took out the cigarettes and put them on the bench. Finally, as his hands patted my legs, he noticed that my calves were square. I pulled more cigarettes out.

"We have a problem, *Licenciado,*" he said as he looked over at the stack of seven packs of cigarettes. "Maybe you should empty everything." I took out three more packs of cigarettes and my micro cassette tape recorder, placing them on the bench. Hey, how else was I supposed to get quotes for this book? All the fancy import-export and open border laws hadn't been passed yet and a small tape recorder like that was worth a lot of money in Mexico. He grabbed it, turned it over, and touched buttons. "Does it play music?" I shook my head. "These are prohibited inside. Sir," he looked at me sternly. "I don't think that you really smoke that much. We definitely have a problem. What are we going to do? Smuggling..."

A deal was struck after stooping and hand waving: he got three packs of cigarettes and all my change while Bravo agreed to keep the tape recorder inside his desk drawer, next to a thirty-eight-caliber pistol, at least until we came out. Luckily, the guard never even came close to my stash of bills for more bribes. Lord knows we would need them.

We were directed down a half flight of stairs to an open area in the center of the building where uniformed guards searched bags on top of an aluminum table. Food thumped and dishes clanked. "Not permitted," was repeated many times over. There were discussions and handshakes. Fernando paid extra to get the oranges in.

Next, we were directed down a flight of stairs to a tunnel. Even with Fernando next to me, it felt mighty lonely. I couldn't help but daydream about Greek mythology that we had studied in grade school. As our steps echoed within the narrow tunnel, I felt as if we were passing over the River of Styx to the underworld. Only problem was that nobody ever came back.

The tunnel ended facing a huge metal door with a metal sliding peephole. Four uniformed guards stood alongside a cement counter. This was the final passage. Fernando's identification was checked and placed into a wall mounted wooden cubbyhole. The guard handed Fernando a plastic chip with a number painted on it, then waved him on to the other end of the counter where the back of his hand was stamped with invisible ink. I handed the guard my identification.

"Expired," he said, handed it back and bent down to brush his boots. I handed him Bravo's note. He read it and shrugged his shoulders while Fernando waited.

"It's hot down here," said Fernando. "Don't you guys have a pop machine?"

The guards laughed and agreed that it was hot. Caution should not be too cautious. I reached down into the top of my socks for a folded soda pop bill, most naturally After my identification was properly stored and my plastic chip was in my pocket with the special card given at the door and the back of my hand was stamped, one guard heaved on the door handle. It clanged. Then he and another guard pulled while the hinges squeaked and sunlight filled the room

Once we stepped out, the door slammed behind us. We were alone in an open courtyard surrounded by tall, concrete, cellblocks. The courtyard was a maze of concrete planters and different levels of cement paths with steps, but no signs, no guards. Fernando and I walked up and back, searching for numbers like lost puppies until a prisoner walked past and pointed.

We found four men dressed in freshly pressed imported suits. One sat on a concrete bench reading a newspaper while a prisoner shined his boots. The other three stood next to an open set of doors. The backs of their jackets bulged. They gossiped about women. Fernando asked for C block visiting room and the guy with the paper made a motion by tugging one end of his newspaper.

Inside the doors, we found concrete stairs leading up. At the top of the stairs in a small office with an electric heater whose coils glowed orange, another man dressed in a suit asked who we wanted to see. "It's not his visiting day," he said which started Fernando to stooping and waving and both of us to digging in our pockets. This guard said no after three handshakes. A prisoner came in with some kind of a message and the guard left.

21

"Jesús LaCierba?" asked the prisoner after the guard left. "He's a good man. Just sit down out here," he said leading us out to some concrete benches in a hall that faced counters. "I'll take care of things with the guard. He owes me." A family ran up to the cement counter and leaned across to hug a man whose lined eyes filled with tears. Farther down, a woman handed a man a bag of *tortillas* and another bag full of *nopales.* There were kisses and hugs. Even though guards stood nearby, off to one side, it was like a homecoming.

Fernando bought a pack of chewing gum from a prisoner who walked with a shoe box full of candy and gum hanging from his neck about the time that the prisoner who led us out to the hall told me to go back into the office and try again. He told me he did all he could and now it required handshakes. The guard inspected my hand under a black light. He looked suspiciously at my plastic chip and card before we shook hands. He told me that everything would be arranged and please just sit in the hall.

Even though he had lost weight, we recognized Chucho's straight black hair, hanging down over his forehead and his droopy mustache. The guard marched him in while pointing to an empty counter. He tapped Chucho's shoulder and walked over to one corner.

"How?"

"Lorenzo is your lawyer today."

"As your lawyer, I have good news and bad." We emptied our pockets on the counter. Out of the twenty packs of cigarettes, we managed to get fifteen in. Then we held up the plastic bags full of food and clumped them on the counter.

"The good news is that we bring gifts," said Fernando.

"The bad news is that I haven't moved your paperwork yet."

Chucho laughed. He stared at Fernando and extended his hand. They shook and Chucho's eyes got moist and red as he said, "We haven't always seen things the same way..."

22

Course, Fernando and I took to babbling until Chucho laughed again. "It's good to see you both," he said pumping Fernando's hand, then mine. "I'm embarrassed by my circumstances."

Chucho had made very good friends. While the other visitors were shooed away every ten minutes, we kept talking and talking. We talked about weddings, family, cars, the weather and even the subway. A guard touched Chucho's shoulder and we shook hands again. "My regards to your families."

We passed each one of the same checkpoints on the way out, at the office alongside the visiting area, then outside on the steps where another guard in a suit had sat down for a shoeshine. Fernando clinked his keys on the giant metal door. Inside, our hands were put under a black light. Our identification was exchanged for our chips. Upstairs we were frisked again before I shook Bravo's hand and he returned my tape recorder. At the door, we handed our colored cards to the man in the rumpled uniform.

Outside, the sun seemed very bright and the air tasted sweet. Back in Fernando's taxi, we both lit a cigarette. Fernando looked out the windshield blankly before turning the key. The car vibrated lightly, then lurched forward

Fernando told me that we'd better take a look at Manolo's car that same day. "Working on cars is more fun than driving in this smog," he said.

An hour later, Fernando and I jacked up the big eight-cylinder Mustang, carefully sweeping aside the almost white doggy dungs. We crawled underneath and took the starter motor off. Then, we crawled back out to take that bad boy apart.

"This is the original," said Fernando, breaking the seals. "Steel: the new ones are made of aluminum."

There was a short somewhere in the hundreds of feet of copper wiring contained in the tiny motor. I asked Fernando what a rebuilt motor might cost.

"It's cheaper just to exchange this inner assembly for a rewired section. The casing of this motor is worth money. We don't want to give it up."

In Fernando's taxi, we drove across town to pick up some new points and the rewired section of the motor. After thirty minutes of driving, Fernando entered a tiny one-way street, parked in front of a dilapidated wooden building. It was one room that measured twelve by fifteen feet. Three young men worked at a crude wooden bench with vices, pliers and files, stripping old wire and restringing them under the guidance of the electrical *maestro*. We traded in the old one and gave a few dollars for a restrung one.

Back at my mother-in-law's, the restrung section of motor didn't fit quite right. The higher you climb, the more rocks you have to dodge. Fernando devised a set of washers and fit it all back together. He tested the spring action and shook his head. We took it all apart again. He invented something else. We climbed upstairs to the kitchen and Fernando took a metal rod out of his tool kit. Course, the women didn't see the kitchen strewn with greasy tools. We carefully moved Margarita's recently married sister's postcard to one side, next to a fruit bowl. With the toaster covered, Fernando heated the rod over the stove like a blacksmith and soldered the thing-a-ma-jig good and plenty.

Downstairs, it all fit together. Fernando turned the key and the engine cranked on the first try, throwing a black diesel smelling cloud into the air. "This took longer," said Fernando, sticking his head out of the open car window, "It must have been impossible."

Jeff Benik

The Hondurans had a hard time with "Jeff" and ended up calling him "Chaff." Even decades after our Peace Corps experience, sometimes I called him Chaff and sometimes, Jeff. Likewise, "Larry" always came out "Lahrrie" so we compromised on Lorenzo. About the only thing Jeff Benik and I had in common was that we were both young unemployed westerners, he from the Bay Area in California and I from the Phoenix metro area in Arizona. Benik's mother was an Austrian immigrant who had survived the Nazi death camps while my ancestors were Central European Catholics. The first time we met (before going native), he wore blue denim bell bottom trousers, an orange t-shirt with "Oakland Athletics" across his chest and Mexican sandals without socks. I wore cowboy straight legged blue denim, a plaid long sleeved collared shirt with breast pockets and construction boots. We both had long hair and beards, his dark and mine light. Chaff, a former high-school all-star baseball player, stood over six feet while I was a healthy five feet nine inches. He was an outdoorsman. I was a book worm. We looked like Mutt and Jeff from the funny pages and sometimes bickered like old spinsters in pancake make-up but God, could he make me laugh.

Our paths to Tegucigalpa in November, 1975 were a bit different but both were blazed by others. Following Watergate, the U.S. Congress began a series of investigations and a reformation of foreign policy. One of the consequences was a hearing held by the Senate Securities and Exchange Commission which exposed bribes from U.S. owned fruit companies to the Honduran President. Days later, Juan Melgar Castro and the military took over the government. According to the United Nations, only Haiti surpassed Honduran poverty in the western hemisphere. The United States began to increase loans and expertise for that nation's development. Between 1975 and 1982, Honduras experienced enormous investments in infrastructure. Chaff was recruited to teach industrial arts for the first time in a new high school. My job was to help with a new general city plan, the precursor to infrastructure construction.

Following training, we were both assigned to the Caribbean Coast, La Ceiba, which was a fruit port. The Hondurans had a saying, "In Tegucigalpa we study. In San Pedro Sula we work and in La Ceiba, we party." After landing, the taxi driver passed a huge billboard with a cropped photo of an extremely buxom dark-skinned woman clad in the tiniest of bikinis. The photo began at her shoulders and included her trunk to the knees, a curvaceous body with complimentary lines of perspiration running down her flat stomach and down the inside of her legs. In one hand she nonchalantly held a sweating amber colored beer bottle resting on her ample hip. The caption read, "The dark one with body." I knew that I would like this place.

Wedged between deep green jungle canopied mountains and the blue Caribbean Sea, La Ceiba was built on a narrow fertile plain, thick with banana, pineapple, orange and grapefruit trees, farmed by an American company since 1932. I would find out shortly that all of Honduras's third most populated city was funded by that same company; streets, water, sewer, storm drainage and even the electric lines. Unfortunately, nobody in the capital knew where the underground services were located or, their sizes. All new infrastructure was funded via the national, not local government and the fruit companies were on their way out. My job was to find, map and describe.

Our shops were unusual. Chaff was taken to a huge classroom stacked almost to the ceiling with wooden crates containing electric band saws, lathes, belt sanders, hand tools and huge benches. There were no cabinets, no wall mounted peg boards, no painted safety lines on the floors, just stacks of crates in an unairconditioned warehouse-like room. I reported to city hall where the city engineer, his survey crew chief, a secretary and a Peace Corps volunteer civil engineer were jammed into a closet-like room. There was no space for even another chair let alone a table. Chaff talked to the principal and recruited a team of high school students to help him. The Peace Corps civil engineer and I met with the mayor who promised us another office.

My formative years had been in the desert and tropical heat was difficult to get used to. In Arizona, perspiration felt like water but in the tropics it felt oily. There was a lot of sweat in La Ceiba even though we arrived during the "dry" season. Daily high temperatures were rising quickly, mid-eighties, then mid-nineties. The humidity was often more than eighty percent and both of us returned to our borrowed digs with our clothing soaking wet: Chaff from working in an oven-like warehouse and I from walking the streets under direct tropical sun while marking maps. I don't remember Chaff ever complaining.

One day he hunted me down during the daytime on his new three speed bike. "A teacher at school turned me on to his aunt who has a place to rent. Wanna look?"

Most nicer homes in town were built on stilts made of concrete and rebar. Some (including the one we visited) had a bottom floor constructed with concrete block and an upper floor of wooden interlocking slats. The house we rented was basically an "L" shape with a concrete patio shaded by the overhanging upper floor. There were no windows, just louvered wooden slats, no ceiling fans or air-conditioner. It had two separate entrances. One led into a street-side small bedroom which had a door that led to a living room. The second entrance led to a small kitchen/dining room, a doored walk-in pantry, bathroom and another doorless small bedroom. The flat had electricity and indoor plumbing. The price was right. That's when I found out that Chaff definitely had a habit.

"Let's flip for the room with the door," he said.

Chaff didn't know that I avoid gambling. I am a sore loser. "Sure." I pulled out a Honduran coin. "Call it."

"Heads."

It was tails. "My bed will go there," I said, pointing. "The other entrance will be our front door." I slid the coin back into my pocket.

"*Alta cocker.*"

"What?"

"Yiddish. I thought you were educated. Two outa three?" Chaff pulled his own coin out and showed me both sides. He lost again. "Three outa five?"

"*Dreck* on you. That's German. Talk to Sandy and Dee Dee. Maybe they could help you make a curtain."

And they did! I didn't know it yet, but Sandy and Chaff had become a "thing." It would last for more than four decades. He never complained to me. So, we had a flat with a curtain on one door and the rest was completely empty. The first few days we ate standing up and slept on the concrete floors in sleeping bags. It took quite a few toe-touches just to get mobile. Someone offered Chaff an old beat-up table for the kitchen. We bought a two-burner propane cooking stove and two bottles of propane. I found a carpentry shop about a mile from our new place and ordered another new table and four chairs. Once they were delivered by a horse drawn wagon, we could at least sit down and eat. Next, we asked the same carpenter to build some cane chairs, a cane sofa and a tiny bedside table for my room. I found an army cot at a local hardware store and Chaff built his own king-size bed, using foam for a mattress. The most difficult piece was refrigeration for our food. Tiny apartment refrigerators were imported and cost good and plenty. Someone donated an old wooden ice box lined with tin. The outside was painted red and you could still read the Coca Cola mark on the front. We alternated taking a taxi once every five days to buy a fifty-pound block of ice.

Our lives became simpler than back home; no radio, television or phone. The only person I knew in town who had a telephone was the mayor in his office. If you needed to talk to anyone, you walked to their home or place of business. Our only connection to the outside world was the local newspaper in Spanish that always included photos of pretty girls in bikinis on page one. Each day, Chaff rode off early in the morning, pedaling three or four miles to his school. I walked about two miles to an old warehouse that had been refurbished into a two-room office space. We returned before noon about the time a round black woman in a print dress walked down our street yelling, "*Pescado! Pescado!*" while carrying a basket of fresh fish on her head. Sometimes we bought beef at the local market where aproned butchers stood in puddles of blood, sawing and hacking while kicking at stray dogs. The big treat was the fact that we could now wash our own food and eat salad without fear of disease. We usually stripped down to our undies, took turns cooking, ate, took a delicious nap, showered and changed clothes before returning to work. Lunch time was three hours long on the Honduran Caribbean Coast. A neighbor woman offered to wash our clothes at an incredibly low price. Every three days, one of her sons came by to pick up the dirty stuff and the next morning a box was placed on our doorstep with clean clothing, folded. The drawback was that she washed it in a river and soon, buttons came off, tiny worn spots appeared. Our wardrobe began to change as clothes wore out. We bought *guayaberas* and hats. I had a woman cut my hair short like a German sailor while Dee Dee trimmed Chaff's dark mane and we both trimmed our beards down with scissors.

"What the hell kinda haircut is that? You a member of the Aryan Brotherhood?"

"Before Dee Dee cut your hair, I thought you were going for that famous rabbi look. What's his name? Oh yeah, Jesus."

In less than ninety days, we had gone native and our language skills improved. Learning a new language is influenced by both age and personality. Older volunteers seem to struggle more. Shy volunteers also have problems. In our cases, shy did not fit. I had a bit of an advantage. Before reporting to the Peace Corps, I spent five weeks in Mexico City on my dime, studying Spanish and courting Margarita, a beautiful Mexican maiden. Chaff, who liked physical humor, showed up cold but certainly made up for lost time. When he spoke Spanish, he exaggerated his facial and body expressions like a mime. He also learned Honduran slang at work in the classroom, sometimes with unexpected results. He had been told that the word "*Puchica*" meant "cool." He used it often until we found out it was really vulgar.

One day at work, the secretary escorted a chunky middle-aged Honduran back to my office and introduced himself as her husband. I stood to shake his hand.

"Do you play basketball?" he asked in Spanish. He coached the local Coca Cola team.

Within forty-eight hours, Chaff and I reported to a middle school gym a few blocks from our house, ready to play. The coach introduced us to a young team, mostly shorter than me. He explained that the added height should help, me as a power forward and Chaff as a center. Once we began to scrimmage, it was obvious that these youngsters only understood run and gun: no plays, no defense and no rebounding. A smoker, I was soon blowin' like a bull snake at a barking dog. We practiced for about an hour. Dark outside, the entire team insisted on accompanying us home.

One block from the gym, we passed a one-story clapboard home with a neon beer sign in a window that had been shuttered an hour earlier.

Chaff motioned for the team to enter. "I'm paying," he explained in Spanish.

The group stopped. Some of the young men had looks of horror on their face. "Our mothers would kill us if they found out!" That's when we discovered they were all under eighteen years of age. They all had to go home and do homework.

Back at our place, Chaff pushed aside the living room cane chairs and cane love seat and laid down on the concrete. "What are you doing?"

"My back is killin' me. Can you please get me the blue pill jar next to my bed?"

He popped two pills. "What's that?"

"Valium. In high school I fell forty feet flat on my back while rappelling with a friend off of the side of a hill."

"What the hell are you playing basketball for?"

"We only live once, Lorenzo."

Eventually, Chaff invited the team to our house on Saturday afternoons where he taught them how to play poker. Since they were all poor, we bet with soda bottle caps. Chaff christened each member of the team with a nickname which they enjoyed. They christened him the "cuckolded lion."

Within weeks, the team began to suspect cheating as Chaff accumulated a box full of bottle caps. First, they found aces up his sleeves and made him play bare chested. Next, someone noticed that he occasionally reached in his sock. The team jumped him, laughing, held him down and took off his socks to find more cards. Chaff got up and acted insulted. Everyone laughed louder. Within two months, the entire team became expert at cheating. Who says that the Peace

Corps serves no purpose? We supply some of the best teachers in the world!

Unfortunately, our basketball did not improve much. We never could match La Blanquita soap factory's team. They were taller and older. They could also trap, steal, rebound and shoot: a deadly combination. Chaff was personally absolved once he played with his high school's faculty against the varsity soccer team. It was broadcast over our local radio station. Midway through the game, the announcer screamed, "*Goooooooooooolllllll! El gringo metió un golazo!*"

During one vacation, Chaff met his parents in Jamaica. He came home with a radio/tape recorder, dozens of reggae tapes and a horse race form. I learned his preferred gambling was on the ponies.

Our paths separated once La Ceiba's first General Plan was presented and adopted. The Peace Corps transferred me to the capital to help with a different program. While there, my Mexican maiden and her mother showed up for a visit during a Peace Corps Spanish workshop that both Sandy and Chaff were attending. My future mother-in-law, Socorro or Choco as the family called her, was a very formal person. For some reason, Chaff had a hard time with the name "Choco" and called her "Chancho" which means male pig. The group was flabbergasted until Chaff began his physical humor, bobbing and weaving his way out of his *faux pas*. Choco burst out laughing and hugged him.

Years later after we had all reverted to our Christian names, Sandy, Jeff, Margarita and I all ended up in California. Jeff and Sandy attended my sons' christenings where we partied without poker since Jeff was wearing a dangerous suit and shirt with long sleeves. Our middles widened. Our hair changed color and began to fall out. Jeff bought an interest in a race horse and briefly rode high as it won over and over until breaking a leg. Once, he and I watched the Bay Meadows races and another time I accompanied him and two of his race horse buddies south, following the circuit. They tried to teach me how to handicap.

As Sandy and Jeff raised their girl and we our boys, the social events became more complex to arrange. About three or four times a year, we drove to their place and spent a night or two, watching horse races on television, swimming, eating and singing. Jeff and Sandy became adopted uncle and aunt. When my boys were teenagers, they disappeared upstairs with Jeff.

"Where are the boys?" I asked.

"Oh, they're upstairs. Jeff is showing them his office."

In the company of my friend, laughter was the sound. It was too quiet. I snuck upstairs and tip-toed into the office where the three were watching a computer screen. I could hear a female voice saying, "Just like I like it: one in the pink and one in the stink."

"Chaff!"

He immediately feigned surprise and turned off the computer while my boys looked down. "It was an anatomy lesson, Lorenzo."

His health took a bad turn. First it was hip replacement. Then I believe, knee replacement. Finally, he noticed that he was having problems raising his arms above his head when putting on a t-shirt. He went to therapy. It worsened. They operated on his back. It worsened. He changed specialists.

"Mr. Benik, you have Lou Gehrig's disease."

I went to three group support sessions with him. By the last, he was in a wheelchair and those who had been at the first meeting were all gone. The last time I saw him, the women all took a drive so we could talk. He had problems holding his head up while seated in his wheelchair, rocking back and forth. He wore a sort of microphone that amplified his voice.

"I've been thinking about horse racing and the Peace Corps," he whispered.

"How are they related?"

"I liked horse races 'cause of the handicapping exercise. It was fun figuring out how a horse might run on a certain day given the weather, the track conditions, the rider and the competition. It reminded me of our government and the Peace Corps. They handicapped different countries. In the end, you win some, you lose some."

Rafael Iglesias Bermudez

Urban Planning was a popular graduate program in Mexico City's U.N.A.M., so popular that the officials doubled the number of candidates and divided us into two groups of forty. By 1977 George Bush Senior's off-shore oil rigs set up in the Gulf were now producing, resulting in an incredible cash cow for Mexico. The government was spending more on infrastructure than it had in the entire twentieth century and building requires builders. The government had literally just moved this department from a tiny downtown office to the University City's architectural tower next to the dentistry building and kitty-corner to the law quadrangle. It was an exciting place. During the day, the law area was a mass of tables selling used and new books, many of which I had never seen before. There were books by Friedrich Engels, Karl Marx, Fidel Castro, Che Guevara and even Mao. I had read a few of these authors back home but was unaware that they had written so many books. There were also lots of carts selling hotdogs, steaming corn on the cob and *taquitos*. There were folks walking around selling kites, weaving through the crowds of youngsters talking, eating and even singing. It was common to find musical groups playing before passing the hat.

Our program was set up for working professionals so the classes were offered at night. By the time we arrived past six, the crowds, book tables and food carts were gone. There was a lone outside snack bar near the architectural entrance. Don Pepe ran it, sometimes with the help of his young son. The wiry tattooed man with curly dark hair wore cotton trousers, a t-shirt and a long butcher's apron. He sweat as he worked the grill, cooking up tacos, pouring coffee but he always had a kind smile and talked. He remembered our names and referred to us by our titles like *arquitecto*, *licenciado* or *ingeniero*. Like in the United States, the graduate program consisted of an eclectic crew of lawyers, engineers, architects and even a few students (like me) with a degree in sociology. Many of the students were married with children. Since the Mexican work week demanded forty-eight hours, studying at night was especially difficult for those with children.

My living situation was precarious. By the time classes started, I had already moved three times and was looking again. On the third-floor hall of the architecture tower, we had a student bulletin board where I saw a note with a telephone number. "Foreign graduate student seeks roommate."

The voice had a different accent. Our program had five foreigners: two Brazilians, two Colombians, and me. Rafael was one of the Colombians. We agreed to meet downtown in front of Bellas Artes which was easily accessible by the subway and near some apartments Rafael wanted to check out. Arriving early, I turned up my collar, took one glove off and bought a cup of hot coffee from a street vendor before taking a seat on a concrete planter. Rafael had only said that he would be easy to spot in an orange scarf. Large groups of people walked up the stairs to disperse in different directions every few minutes. A very tall thin man walked briskly up the stairs dressed flamboyantly in an Eisenhower type of jacket and very long orange scarf, wrapped twice around his neck.

"Lorenzo?" We shook hands and walked towards the famous Sanborns restaurant about a block away, talking. When I stumbled over a word in Spanish, he immediately switched to English. He was fluent. When the topic turned to literature, he talked at length about Hemingway, Fitzgerald, London, Kerouac, Miller, Brautigan, Joyce and more. Within minutes it was obvious that this man was much better educated than I. He was also noticeably effeminate.

We squeezed onto two open stools at the counter. The neatly dressed businessman next to Rafael turned to sneer at his jacket and scarf. We ordered coffee and rolls, comparing stories about the program, the instructors, living and working in Mexico City. The man next to Rafael occasionally made rude sounds. We continued to talk, ignoring him.

"*Pinche joto,*" (damn queer) he mumbled.

Rafael swiveled the stool to face him. "*Me encanta cuando me hablas así, guapo.*" (I love when you talk to me like that, handsome.) The businessman's jaw slackened. He quickly reached into a pocket and pulled out some pesos which he threw on the counter. He grabbed his briefcase and nearly ran to the door, looking back at Rafael one more time, his face still in shock.

"He sure made that easy," said Rafael and I burst out laughing.

Rafael had a list of apartments, supplied by one of his new Mexican real estate friends. Neither of us had a car so it was all buses and walking which gave me time to think about how complicated and awkward it would be living with someone who brought boyfriends home instead of girlfriends. The first flat might have been the best with about 800 square feet, a working bathroom, kitchen, living room and two bedrooms.

"It's noisy," I said. We headed to another. By three in the afternoon, after visiting four apartments, Rafael said, "It's getting late. I have some more to look at tomorrow. I can call if I find something."

He found a small place downtown in the neighborhood known as La Merced, near the Fray Servando subway station. The building was very old and you had to climb three floors but the price was right. I found a weird place on the roof of a three-story building a few blocks from a subway station. It really had been four cell-like rooms for maids where the owner had removed two walls to create two long narrow adjoining rooms with a door between. It was a bit like living in a submarine. The bathroom was a separate structure in the middle of the roof. Floor, ceiling and walls were all tiled. My shower was a simple galvanized pipe sticking out. Next to it was a toilet. This meant when it rained, I had to dart through a shower to get to a shower. Like Rafael's place, it was cheap.

He invited me over on a Saturday for an early luncheon with a Mexican journalist, a Colombian photographer and a Brazilian architect. Rafael had bought a cheap pine table and chairs with twine backing and seats. He had painted these with primary colors in a most folkloric manner. He bought a used love seat and covered it with a white sheet. There were plants and the walls were all painted different colors, looking like something out of an architectural magazine except he had done it with next to no money.

Rafael was quite the host. He sat us in his tiny living room, serving us drinks, while he scurried back to the kitchen. We had an animated conversation about current events, construction, art and places to see in the America's oldest continually inhabited city. I sat on the edge of my chair as we talked until Rafael announced, "*Ya está la comida*" (Food's ready). He had prepared a three-course meal like in a restaurant. He actually had matching plates.

"I picked them up in the thieves' market," he deadpanned in English.

We were still talking as the sun began to set. The journalist looked out a window and mentioned that it was best to head for the subway before dark. Everyone nodded.

Both Rafael and I picked up cash by working illegally as English teachers (we had student visas). He also picked up some side jobs with architects from time to time. Life got very complicated and busy after a professor at the university recruited me to work in a large engineering and construction firm. They hired me on a short-term basis to create the basis for a socio-economic impact statement about the construction of large boulevards and extensions of the subway system which would result in the demolition of 20,000 homes over the next eighteen months. That implied about 100,000 homeless city-wide. This meant that I would be working forty-eight hours a week as well as attending classes each night and doing all the homework. I learned to get by on four hours a night sleep. There wasn't time to be social.

That's how I stumbled upon the plight of Santa Anita, only about a mile east of my roof-top bachelor pad. Over the next few months, I wrote a study outlining how to measure the impact by using an affected zone near my apartment (La Moderna) as the control where very few families were affected and Santa Anita as the test area. I visited the neighborhoods and interviewed local leaders. Using aerial photography, I estimated that five hundred families or three thousand five hundred people would be displaced. Almost immediately, I noticed that the east side of the Santa Anita was bordered by a strange diagonal boulevard (Coyuya). Some research revealed that during the revolutionary period (1910-1928), it had been a railroad line. I inferred that the boulevard must have a decent base in order to support the rails. The remainder of the neighborhood had been a floating island five hundred years before, upon which the Aztecs grew a coarse straw used for brushes and brooms (*zacate*). Originally, it was called Zacatlamanco Huehuetl. This remaining area would require substantial excavation and fill to support the new overhead tracks planned to cross through the middle of the neighborhood. I also noticed that it was suspiciously close to an existing light rail line to the west (near my apartment), one mile. Usually when planning such lines, more than a mile and a half between lines is recommended. A detour to the east would have made it possible to extend the line further south in the future. The planned line would eventually have to stop on the other side of a river (Rio Churubusco). In other words, a detour would cost less to build, affect fewer citizens and serve better. I took my preliminary findings to my boss.

He told me in Spanish, "I personally walked Santa Anita. It's full of fucked up poor people living in squalor. Best we knock it all down. Listen: your job is to find out why this is a good idea, not post detour signs and slow us down."

I finished the report per the contract and included five alternative routes for detours around the historic Santa Anita. Then, I quit and went back to teaching English part-time. Within a month, one of my classes assigned a project about housing. During a class break, I approached my two favorite team members Roberto LaValle and Hugo Rosas Relo, an architect and an engineer but I had one caveat: we needed Rafael Iglesias Bermuda in the group. He had recently switched to our large group of students.

"He's a butterfly," said Hugo diplomatically, glancing across the room at Rafa, dressed in a pair of his tight leather pants and angora pullover sweater, waving dramatically as he spoke to another group.

"He's the smartest guy in this class."

Rafa accepted and the professor approved the idea with this warning: be careful of political topics. The university will not back you if there is a problem. You will be on your own. Foreigners could even be deported. That was Rafa and me.

Since I had experience with random sample surveys, I wrote a five-page questionnaire. It was to be administered by one of our team since many of the residents were illiterate. The first part had to do with the construction of the home. Many involved squatters living in homes constructed of discarded tin, wood and even cardboard. The team member could judge the materials while he sat with the family, taking notes. The vast majority of the questions had to do with life-style: types of education, employment, wages, number of family members, etc. We divided the neighborhood into four zones based upon my experiences. We also immediately discarded the professor's warning by creating an official looking badge with a photo, name, and the university emblem. Who would talk to us if we couldn't even identify ourselves?

We had to agree on the questionnaire. This was not easy. At one meeting, Roberto, normally a calm man, got worked up about danger and started to insult me. Overworked and stressed, I lost my temper, grabbed his shirt with one hand to pull him closer and cocked the other arm. Before I could deliver, Rafa clinched me from behind, whispering, "*Calmate machito*" (Easy my little macho). We worked it out. Roberto had been a prophet. I found out later that one family I visited actually voted whether or not to kill me, fearing that I was some sort of government swine. The elder mother cast the deciding vote telling them, "*Vamos a darle al güero una oportunidad primero,*" (We are going to give blondie a chance first). Over time, they became steadfast friends.

Within a couple of months, we had more information about who lived in Santa Anita than the government. I kept in contact with the local leaders and one invited me into his house. He very formally offered me a seat and fetched a folded personal invitation to a meeting sponsored by the government to discuss the impending expropriation of lands to facilitate the construction of roads and elevated light rail. He quizzed me. Once I explained my former employment and university studies, he invited me to accompany him.

"I'm on a student visa and am not supposed to get involved with politics."

"You will just accompany me as a guest."

The night of the meeting, I dressed in a sport coat and tie. Held in the neighborhood kindergarten, it was by invitation only. Outside the door, several hundred people, many dressed in rags, listened, passing word to the crowd about what was happening inside. Armed guards at the door denied me entrance but inside, Don Goyo saw me and motioned to them with a wave. I was led to the front to sit at a table with a microphone in front of a make-shift stage where five men in suits sat. One was my former boss.

Don Goyo gave a very formal statement, mostly about himself and then abruptly passed his microphone to me introducing me as his "urban planner." I introduced myself and explained that a group in the national university had studied the case of Santa Anita. I described some of the findings and then mentioned the five alternative detours that should cost less, affect fewer people and serve the public better. I ended with a question, *"¿Podrían hacer comentarios sobre las alternativas? (Could you comment on these alternatives?)*

The five looked at each other quizzically. My former boss covered a microphone with one hand and whispered in the ear of a man next to him. He nodded. *"Don Goyo. Invitaremos a Ud. y a su grupo a juntarse con nuestro grupo para discutir el asunto. Le mandaremos a Ud. la fecha y la hora apropriada. Con eso, terminamos la discusión* (Don Goyo. We will invite your group to meet with our group to discuss this. We will send you an invitation with the date and time. With that, we close tonight's discussion). They all got up and left.

Don Goyo slunk out quickly. As I turned to make my way with the crowd, a man who looked like a middle-aged John Steinbeck offered his hand and introduced himself. We walked together as he talked non-stop about his neighbors and how they would like to talk to me. Before I could demur, his mother, an older woman with white hair covered by a shawl, took my arm, smiling and said, *"Ven güerito. Tenemos galletas y café."* (Come on blondie. We have cookies and coffee).

I ended up helping them for nearly two and one half years. They formed a formal group and eventually hired a consulting Mexican urban planner as well as a Mexican lawyer who won their case on appeal, becoming locally famous. However, Roberto and our instructor's warnings were valid. The government began to play hardball: removing the judge and retrying the case ÷ reversing the decision, water cutoffs electric cutoffs, knocking down buildings with residents still in them, attempted bombings, and attempted kidnappings. At one meeting, the Delegado (Burrough Chairman) warned. "I'll get you out of here even if It's feet first."

During this same time period, a medium sized engineering firm hired me and I soon found a spot for Rafa. Sometimes, we worked side by side at drafting tables in a large room manned by fifteen draftsmen. He was a talker and loved to tease me, especially if I looked glum. One day, heads down inking maps next to one another, he started in English because none of the draftsmen spoke it.

"Lorenzo. I have a new boyfriend. He is young and firm…"

"I don't wanna hear 'bout it."

"Last night I grabbed him from behind…"

"Not interested."

"And I pulled his pants down…"

"STOP!"

The one word in English that all the draftsmen knew was "stop" and they did, politely looking up at me for the next instruction. *"Perdón. Perdón,"* I said and waved at them to continue while Rafa howled.

They tried to kidnap me three times. The last time, I went underground before escaping north. The only reason that I knew anything about going underground was due to some published interviews with American folks on the run. I understood that one had to cut all ties with family, friends and to keep moving. The first two days and nights on the streets were difficult. The third night I slipped into an industrial zone where an architect friend of mine had a small office we sometimes used for other projects. The office had a shower, toilet and a tiny sofa. So long as I left no trace and left early in the morning, even my friend would not realize that I was sleeping there.

After a few days, it was time to find a new hide-out. I called Rafa at work. "Where have you been? My joke wasn't that bad." he said.

I explained the situation to the Santa Anita veteran. Of course, he offered me his place. "There's a dragnet out for me. They've already put my house and my mother-in-law's house under surveillance. They've started interrogating my in-laws and soon will start with every place I've worked in the last few years. All the Santa Anita phones are tapped. It has to be a person you know but I do not."

"Call me back tomorrow. Same time."

This is when I saw a different side of Rafa. Helping me could have resulted in his own deportation or even worse. The next day, he reported. "Come by the office. I'll leave a note with Berta. It contains the name and address of a Colombian friend, an architect. She's studying a master's because she needed to leave the country. Her brother was a member of FARC (a Colombian revolutionary group). They caught him, beat him until he could no longer stand, then shot him in the head before interrogating his family and friends.

We both made it home. I escaped to the U.S.A. and Rafa eventually went home to accept a job in a Colombian university as an instructor.

Will James

Will worked from two thirty in the afternoon until midnight and the class ran from nine in the morning until noon so he usually spent some time rubbing his eyes and blinking while the adult education instructor lectured. We were the only two men attending and we met at a coffee machine during break, complaining in whispers: our wives had drafted us into service. Very early on, we walked to a parking lot where we could talk freely without women eavesdropping. What did we talk about? Baseball mostly.

Will's daughter was the same age as my older of two boys. The class was a pre-pre school for children while also offering a class on parenthood. The routine was to meet in a classroom where parents and children sang together. This was followed by children and parents' group projects. Older children (three and four-years old) headed off to a supervised playground with one way glass installed on a wall and the younger children were sent to an adjoining supervised playroom with one way glass installed so the children could be observed.

During one of our baseball-talking breaks, I asked Will, "What do you do for a living?" He stammered and said something about a law office. "Oh. You're a lawyer."

"No, no. I supervise a group that revises legal briefs."

"You mean you're an editor?'

"Yes. I've been doing it since university graduation."

Well, I'd never met a professional editor before, just English instructors and secretaries who were good at spelling. I had also just self-published a memoir. "If I bring a copy of my memoir, would you read it?"

"Sure." That was his first mistake, a big one. The very next day I handed him an autographed copy in the parking lot, then pestered him daily. He reported, "I like it. It's a fun read but it could have used more editing."

I pursed my lips and thought for a second. "Are you volunteering to edit the next one?"

"Sure." That might have been the biggest mistake of his adult life.

His wife is the daughter of Chinese immigrants. My wife is an immigrant from Mexico. We started our own cross-cultural adventure. Will took me through the San Francisco Chinatown and made me see with different eyes. He explained the games old men played at the Chinatown light rail stop. He showed me where he got his hair cut for half price. We ate at some places I had only passed and explained how to order, how to eat with chop sticks and what was what.

He also took me to his office on Montgomery Street. Law offices were not my specialty. I'd only been to very few in my entire life. His office was in an old 1920's building. We went into his inner domain, the editing room. A large room with individual tables, the men and women all read silently. Some used markers, others used pens, using printer's notations to mark-up documents because this was before all the computerized programs, before the internet – the stone age of literacy. Some of the editors dressed up like lawyers but others looked much like street people with better haircuts. One lady read sitting straight up. Another man slouched back in his chair and had his feet on the table. There was a set of shelves on one wall full of grammar books, style guides and dictionaries.

"I thought you edited briefs."

"We do but the main part of work involves the evidence: supplemental materials," said Will. From a closet, he pulled out two huge boxes, each full of bound reports. "This is the evidence for one case."

"I'd need a few weeks to even read that," I said.

"Now you're talking!" said one editor. "Weeks? We get days."

"We also rewrite motions, whatever the attorney needs. The truth is that new attorneys do not write well," said Will.

"Where did you learn all this?"

"My major was in English. This was my first real job and I stayed. You learn on the job."

His junior editors were an eclectic lot. They all seemed to have followed different paths. Will took me to a classical music recital of one. However, the downside of such a group was that they were a bit capricious. They changed jobs frequently, leaving Will and the others to carry the load until they could find a substitute.

"It's a bit difficult to find legal editors because it's so specialized," explained Will.

We also started doing things together as families. He and his family attended my younger son's Christening. We took our kids to the park together and attended birthday parties. We all went to Chinese New Year in Frisco with Deanna explaining things. Will and I completed the school year at the adult education center. The teachers and administrators might have been happy to see us go. We did not follow their rules well.

Thirty days later, I flew alone to bush Alaska for a job. My wife never liked cold temperatures and stayed with the children in the Bay Area. Will, Deanna (his wife) and Nicole kept on meeting with my family while I was away for the next eighteen months. They visited zoos, parks, beaches and even camped out.

When anyone talks about Alaska, they mention "cabin-fever." The winter is long and harsh. Going out to play with your dog when the wind-chill factor is fifty-two degrees below zero is never a good idea. Take a dog out for a walk? Fine but do not start running around: you will burn the linings of your lungs. So, I immediately thought about another book. This time I did it right by calling Will before even starting. "Will! I'm thinking about a new book. Were you serious about editing?"

"Sure. What kind of book?"

"Another travel memoir."

"That sounds like a lot more fun than going through hundreds of pages of obscure geology reports for an oil lawsuit or pages and pages of engineering calculations and a bizarre summary that makes no sense for a building lawsuit."

"You guys never do divorces for the rich and famous?"

"No divorces."

In the pre-internet caveman days, I typed up twenty pages and mailed it to Will. Inside was also a self-addressed and stamped envelope for its return. Then, I'd go back to work. Usually, I'd have another twenty pages in a week when his edits appeared at my Alaskan post office box. (We had no home delivery in the bush.) Will used standard printer's notation on the edits which means I had to learn them. They reminded me of short-hand, a lost skillset. By Christmas, we had a book. I flew home for the holidays and visited a local printer who got it all done in California.

While home Will asked, "When's the next book?"

"No. I've had it with writing. It's too much work!"

It didn't take long back in subfreezing temperatures to realize that writing a book was healthier than hanging out in bars or watching television. I called Will. "I've got an idea for another book?"

"I thought you quit."

"I took a vacation. Are you in?"

"Sure."

We followed the same method as before using the post office in charge of photocopies. It worked so well that when I flew home after eighteen months, we had a new book. The same local printer had it printed in weeks.

When I was hired at a new shop, one hundred fifty miles southeast of the Bay Area, Will helped me pack a truck, This was the beginning of a new era in our friendship. The first time he and his family arrived at our home, he noticed my Mexican nylon string guitar which I had been playing on and off without a teacher for more than a decade. He picked it up and plucked strings.

"Do you have a tuning fork?" I handed him one and He tuned the guitar about five times faster than I ever had. Then, he began to play an intricate Beatles song. That's when I found out that he had played guitar since he was fifteen.

He handed it to me. I pulled out a thin folder of beginner tunes, mostly country with three or four cowboy chords.

"Yeah," he said. "That's a good song."

We started going back and forth with visits, carrying guitars. My place had more space and it was easier to concentrate since I had no pets. I bought another steel string guitar from a neighbor. Will convinced me to work more on sevenths and minors and began to preach the gospel of bar chords. Soon, we were playing pop songs and harmonizing with our voices. Our children joined in with percussion. In the beginning a typical visit was arrival on a Saturday, eat, go to some park with the children, eat and play music before watching some children's movie together.

With the invention of the internet, we could literally share books electronically and instantly. Not only that but he no longer had to use the printer's notation since the computer offered us so many alternatives for marking up the written word. I began to write essays and printed them cheaply as pamphlets. This required that I learn about formatting. Will had to pick up on that too. We found computer-based guitar tuners and began to use the internet to find lyrics and arrangement s of songs. This saved an incredible amount of money. Earlier, we had to buy songbooks.

Even the way we attacked music changed. We look at songs and performances on the computer to study them. In caveman days, you had to go see a performance live, preferably in a small venue so that the musician's hands were visible, or listen to records repeatedly until the grooves were worn smooth.

Usually, I typed up the lyrics and noted chords in pencil. Then, based upon the different arrangements we had found online, we began to rearrange it to our liking. An example is an old Hank Williams' tune called "I'm So Lonesome I Could Cry." The Cowboy Junkies, a Canadian group, had this jazzy sounding arrangement with sevenths that Will and I both liked. I did my job and when he arrived for the next visit, we began to experiment, changing a chord here or there.

Will can also play by ear: he listens to someone playing a song and figures out both the melody and the basic chord structure. This is especially handy when we use the computer to find or a song book for an arrangement, then listen to a recording online. "This note and this chord are marked wrong. That's common," Will might say and immediately start fiddling until he got it right.

My neighbor Wayne, a retired grocer, learned to play the guitar at sixty-five. He was a fan of the Nashville sound and had memorized all kinds of nifty riffs. When Will showed up, so did Wayne. We call ourselves the Holiday Way Band. For my fifty-second birthday my wife threw a big wing-ding with friends and family. For the very first time, the Holiday Way Band performed in public.

When we played for fun, at some point, Wayne and Will jam with old country standards like "Wildwood Flower." They take turns doing melody riffs. The three of us play a lot of Merle Haggard and Hank Williams.

My sons went away to college while Will's family grew with the addition of a son and a daughter. The son likes wind instruments and the daughter plays the guitar. Whew! Now we're really cooking with gas. The visits got longer, sometimes three days and changed. There was no need to entertain children anymore. It was music until our fingers hurt, eat and more music."

That's when I noticed that neither Will or I use a pick much. With the guitar body hugging your torso and both hands touching strings, you can feel the vibrations. You become one with the instrument. Will told me that as a youngster, he held the guitar at an angle like a Spaniard and laid an ear on upper bout's side as well.

After one of our very few discussions about grammar, I bought a copy of the *Chicago Manual of Style*. "I'm comma lite," explained Will. Another time when I complained that we had missed some typographical errors in a book, Will responded, "Larry, I'm in my office. On the shelf is the Bible – the Word of God. It too has typos."

So, with the writing, there is no boss, just two guys consorting. Over the past thirty years, Will has edited nineteen of my books, six pamphlets and more than four dozen published articles. Although it ain't the Word of God, how could anyone go wrong with an editor named William James? Musically, Will plays lead while I handle rhythm. We smile more often playing music. It must be good vibrations.

Gloria Jean Link

Bush Alaska is very different. People who live there are usually folks who have been there for many, many generations, or, immigrants from far-off places. The immigrants are usually involved with fishing, lumbering, mining or some governmental service. Dillingham was a regional home to a salmon fleet and two operating canneries at the end of the twentieth century. During the summer months the fishing industry required supplies and Dillingham was its commercial center with a dock, an airport, stores, restaurants, a post office, a bank, a university branch, a high school, a grammar school, a hospital, a radio station, potable water, a sewer system, an electric power generator, a volunteer fire station, eleven churches, two bars and even a Chamber of Commerce. Gloria ran the chamber like playing a fiddle. She knew everybody and got along with them all, maybe partly because she looked Alaskan: big and strong. She was two or three inches taller than me and outweighed me by a lot. Standing next to one another, we appeared like a tree branch alongside a giant tree.

I have never lived anywhere with a population as involved as Dillingham's citizens. Everyone I knew was involved with a group and some with several. Gloria seemed involved with them all. For instance, I arrived in mid-July during the salmon runs when the population triples and everyone everywhere is busy, busy, busy. Gloria almost immediately asked if I played softball. When she found out I was writing a book, she introduced me to some local writers. When she found out I had another published book, she introduced me to the grocery store manager who agreed to put copies on sale via consignment. She introduced me to the local newspaper editor who agreed to print an excerpt as promo.

Her office was a log A-frame on the west side of the Townsite (surveyed in 1947, the portion with water, sewer and electric systems) maybe a block from city hall where I worked. During working hours in the summer, it was always filled with people seated around a Ben Franklin stove, drinking coffee and talking. Gloria had a wood box next to the door filled with kindling. One day I made a mistake by asking, "Who chops your kindlin?"\

Gloria stood up, walked to the box, grabbed her hatchet and held it up. "Do I not look strong enough to chop my own wood, Mr. Lihosit?"

"No, no. I meant..."

"Good," she said, set the hatchet down and smiled.

After work hours, Gloria headed out of town to her trailer. However, she generally went to the Sea View after night meetings to hold court. She was always seated at a long table, filled with men and women. She waved to me and pointed to a seat or someone in the group would get another seat and make a place for me. That's how I met Blackie, an Aleut woman who had been kidnapped by the Japanese during the Second World War invasion and spent years as a "comfort woman." Of her group of Aleuts kidnapped, she was the only one to survive and return. I also met a kindly old gentleman who listened intently but never spoke. One night after he left, I asked Gloria why he never spoke.

"When he was very young, his parents took him and his brother and sister on a picnic near the river. A bear attacked. The father barely had time to put him, the youngest, into a tree. The bear killed and ate his family and he never spoke again."

I met locals from neighboring villages, some with only fifty or sixty inhabitants. They all wore thick-lensed glasses. One evening, I asked about that trait. Gloria looked around and whispered, "During the winter before the river freezes, they are really socked in. There's some incest there."

Gloria's table was always filled with councilmen, store owners, newspaper reporters, bank managers, fishermen, the local chiropractor, anyone and everyone. I think secretly, most of the town wanted to be her "bud." The place was loud. Once in a while, the bartender rang an old bell and the crowd roared because someone had offered to buy everyone a free drink. It was usually a successful salmon boat skipper.

Gloria was also a jokester. One evening at the Sea View, she excused herself to use the rest room. When she came back, she said, "I see you've made friends, California boy." Since I had arrived with short hair and a clean-shaven face, several people in town liked to tease me by calling me that. Most men in town wore shoulder length hair and thick untrimmed beards. Many women wore their hair long and braided.

"Huh?"

"Your name and phone number are on the women's rest room wall with a note – 'for a good time'."

The other women at our table howled and everyone toasted me even though it was not true.

While the other bar in town, the Willow, had a live band playing Thursday, Friday and Saturday nights, the Sea View had a disc jockey and a large karaoke machine Monday through Saturday nights. Set up at one end of the bar with a tiny area railed off for singers, the Sea View also had a large booth bordered by a corner set of picture windows. One of the windows had a view of Nushagak Bay. Even at eleven o'clock at night the sun still shone and you could see whales breaching, playing as they ate salmon. During the summer, it was standing room only and the only way I even got in was by saying, "I'm with Gloria." The huge, tattooed and bearded bouncer nodded and pointed to her table.

The disc jockey always opened his show by playing a Bob Segar favorite called "Old Time Rock N Roll." He sang it as if he were Bob Seger. The audience had menus of songs the machine could accompany. If you wanted to sing, you wrote the name of the song on a slip of paper and put it into the disc jockey's basket. Gloria was not timid. She always sang at least three songs before always heading out with two or three friends about eleven fifteen. These were her "buds."

She had a set net near the mouth of a creek just west of the Townsite. It rose and fell with the tides and if her net was laid across the creek, she was responsible for harvesting the catch. Failure to do so resulted in a stiff fine from our local Alaskan Fish and Game agent. I offered to help but Gloria always reported that she had a team to help harvest and then, on a table under a spotlight outside here trailer, they all cleaned and fileted the fish until two or three in the morning. All five types of salmon migrated up rivers and streams in and around Dillingham. The set nets required a special permit which was posted on a stake. This was considered non-commercial and part of an Alaskan's "right to subsist."

Gloria was also a Catholic. Her favorite joke in the Sea View was to tell me, "See *you* in Confession." The brick church had been built by the parishioners near the airport. There was an anteroom and the sanctuary which was Protestants-like plain. On the far side, behind the altar was a huge picture window. During summer service, we saw pine trees moving with breeze. After the service we always had a pot-luck in a basement. I didn't cook or bake that well yet but Gloria certainly did. Sometimes she brought home-made casserole, or cloud berry pie, or even a German chocolate cake. We ate and talked, sometimes for another hour. It was a small but sincere congregation who was watched over by Father Kelly who flew his own plane in to say Mass.

That first summer, a coffin with the remains of a cannery worker dating back nearly a century was falling from a high bay cliff due to erosion. According to Bob King, the local historian, this had been a Chinese cemetery. There was also a Philippine cemetery. A boot filled with foot bones had been found on the beach. One hundred feet above, a disintegrating wooden coffin stuck out of the cliff. Someone had called the city to help. I heard the radio call from my office and used the city jeep to drive out. It was located almost halfway to the Knakanak Hospital. Public Works employees had already stabilized the coffin with ropes. I hiked uphill and helped to pull the ropes. When the men opened the coffin, we found the remains of a man dressed in a simple suit. His three-foot-long braid was still attached to the skull.

The remains were bagged and brought back to the Townsite. The Dillingham City Mayor Tommy Tilden, a local Native Alaskan, met with the pastors of all the local churches and as a group they decided to rebury the remains. Father Kelly offered a grave site behind the Catholic Church. The Chinese government did not offer re-patriotization for the remains of its citizens from abroad. Since no one knew the man's name or religion, the entire group also decided that all participate.

Gloria and I attended with a group of twenty people. The city had built a new pine coffin and it was lowered with fishing ropes into a new grave dug by Father Kelly with his backhoe. Each pastor made a statement and Tommy even made a moving speech followed by an Elder's ceremony in Yupik.

The coffin incident and unmarked foreign cemeteries piqued my interest. On Saturdays I began to hike down the coast towards the hospital which was built on a cliff overlooking the bay. Originally, it had been a regional orphanage. The 1918 scourge of the Spanish Flu devastated Alaskans. When locals boarded boats to check on Bristol Bay villages up river, they found corpses everywhere and an occasional baby wailing. The disease killed adults and left tiny children unscathed.

The village of Kanakanak, six miles west of the Townsite, was an area wiped out. On one of my hikes all the way to the hospital, built on a tall cliff I noticed groupings of Native Alaskan homes along the beach with the roofs caved in. Gloria had already explained about the epidemic to me and mentioned that the custom was to leave the corpses in their homes, cave in the roof by kicking out support beams and abandoning the village. I touched nothing.

Dillingham is very small. The next day at the grocery store, the mayor stopped me. "I heard you walked to Kanakanak."

"Yes, sir."

"Did you touch anything?"

"No sir. I didn't come here to desecrate graves."

Tommy smiled broadly. "Good for you.". I found out later that the remains of some of his ancestors were there. So were the remains of a former Alaskan First Lady, Bella Gardiner-Hammond. Her husband, former governor Jay Hammond, started as a bush pilot in the Dillingham area.

No-See-Um Day is a special Dillingham holiday. In September, it begins to freeze at night and kills the clouds of mosquitos and no-see-ums, an ultra-tiny flying insect that also bites as it swarms Southwest Alaska during the warm months. Dillingham residents hold an annual fair to celebrate. That year it was held inside the high school due to rain. An incredible number of locals did needlework, made baskets, carved and painted. They set up stalls in the gym to sell their work. With live music, local Native Alaskan dances, speeches and great food like moose stew or reindeer sausages, it was fun. It was also an antidote for the fall blues. The cannery had closed for the season. Most restaurants, and fishing related businesses had closed for the season. No more barges would port until next May or June depending upon the ice. The airlines cut back the scheduled flights. The population dropped from about 6,000 to 2,000 in fifteen days. The sky became dark as millions of birds flew south, abandoning us.

I was there on a two-year contract and Gloria knew I was looking for a keepsake so she introduced me to Sally Small, a Native Alaskan who wove baskets from a local grass and seal guts in the nearby village of Twin Hills. The guts were dyed with natural colors and used to create designs against the light tan colored grass. In order to make the grass malleable, the artist ran it through her teeth to take off a cover layer. Her work was beautiful. However, she did not speak English, only Yupik. Gloria found a translator and we agreed upon a price. I requested that Sally sit with the basket on her lap so I also would have an image of her. She smiled and sat.

Our Halloween parade was interrupted by a white-out snow storm. It got colder. The grocery stores and hardware stores were no longer filled with customers. At Dimitri's restaurant, he closed off half the tables. The library and museum cut hours. Gloria kept working. She talked me into rewriting a historical buildings survey. She worked with the arts council to contract a musician to play for the town folk. At the Sea View, the karaoke machine was covered with a huge plastic dust cover. After night meetings, Gloria and her buds still met.

While it's certainly true that lonely makes friends of strangers, it does not guarantee a lifelong relationship. Even Native Alaskans often moved to Fairbanks or Anchorage to enjoy the big city. Of the outsiders who immigrated for good paying jobs, most eventually left. Often people escape to start anew but change their minds along the way. Gloria, like many others in town, was a bit of a mystery. Little was known about her except that she came from somewhere near Saint Paul, Minnesota.

There's another saying: "When in Rome, do like the Romans." Months of cold weather passed. With the glint of spring, Dillingham celebrated Fur Trading Day. Trappers floated down river with boats and rafts full of beaver, wolf and wolverine pelts. The Dillingham Hotel had a large sign attached to it that read, "Fur Traded." Trappers stacked pelts on the snow in a festive atmosphere. There was interesting food and conversation, bingo games, a beauty contest, a dog sled race, a wet t-shirt and arm-wrestling contests, treats for anyone with cabin fever. One of our planning commissioners, a thin woman, won the women's arm-wrestling division and went on to beat a huge man. The museum director, a curvaceous woman, placed in the wet t-shirt contest. With the rivers opening, fish spawning season was near. I told Gloria, "We should work on a duet for the summer. Nobody sings duets."

"Which song?"

"The Neil Diamond song "You Don't Bring Me Flowers."

"You want me to play Barbara Streisand?"

"I've heard you sing. You can do it."

The internet did not exist yet and Dillingham did not have a music store. I convinced the Sea View owner to turn on the song's video one afternoon when the Sea View was empty. I noted all the lyrics. At Gloria's office, we drank coffee and practiced.

"When we go up to sing, we have to tell the disc jockey what key we want."

"I can't read music."

"Me neither,"

Gloria talked to the owner. "We can practice on Wednesday nights from seven to eight and he will run the machine for us. Nobody's there anyhow."

Our first homework was to figure out in what key we could sing it. The owner tried it in the original key of C. Then, he tried another and another and another. After a half hour, we figured out that E flat would work. Next, we had to work on the ending harmony. Just before the disc jockey reported for duty, we perfected our rendition. I would go up front while Gloria snuck to the bar. I would grab the microphone and begin singing. Within one verse, Gloria would storm up as if angry and grab the microphone out of my hand to sing. After she completed her verse, there would be another microphone in a holder that I could grab and we would alternate. Just before the end, there were a few instrumental bars. We would shrug our shoulders and dance before singing a duet at the end.

On the first night of karaoke, the Sea View was packed. My note to the disc jockey listed the key and a special request: "Call me third." Earlier in the afternoon, he had already been palmed a twenty.

On cue, he said, "Well, this is an unusual request from Larry. A Neil Diamond song. Come on up, Larry!"

Most of the crowd were fisherman or cannery workers who had no idea who I might be. There was no applause, no murmurs. The taped music started and I sang. Gloria stormed the stage and grabbed my microphone, singing her verse and we continued our well-choreographed act. When we finished, the crowd erupted into whistles, foot stomping and yells. They loved the idea of a giant woman giving a small guy hell. We bowed.

A week later while seated at the Sea View with Gloria, she got up earlier than usual. She explained that her set net pickers were all busy that night. "I'll help."

"Can you pick as well as you sing?"

"I always follow big women's orders."

She smiled and motioned for me to follow. We drove to her spot near the mouth of a creek very near the Dillingham salmon fleet dock. She backed her pickup to the edge of what had been water before the tide went out. Now it was a mud flat with a long plastic net twisting and moving as salmon jumped. She left the keys in the ignition and we walked to the back. She handed me a pair of knee-high rubber boots and rubber gloves. I couldn't get the boot on over my own boots.

"Just take off your boots and slip on the rubber ones," she said and pulled a very long, thick plastic fishing rope from the back, laid it out on the ground. One end was already tied to the bumper. "Mud flats can be treacherous. Walk slowly. If you were to sink up to your waist, yell out immediately. I will toss you this rope and use the pickup to pull you out."

"You mean it's like quicksand?"

"Sometimes." She put her hands on her hips. "If anyone should be worried that would be me. I must weigh twice what you do. If I yell, get moving for the truck. That's why the keys are in the ignition. Grab the salmon by the gills. It's easier to balance if you carry one fish in each hand. Just flop them into the pickup bed. Here," she handed me a club. "If they're moving hit them."

We walked to the other side of the creek and began. The net was filled with moving fish, each between twenty-five and thirty pounds. We must have traipsed back and forth dozens of times before one of my boots got caught in the mud. It sank to my knee. I yelled to Gloria.

"That's not bad. Try pulling your foot out of the boot. Then, pull on the boot."

This was successful but one foot and my pants were now covered with sticky mud. We kept working. My arms got very tired and sore before we filled the pickup bed.

"Arms hurt?"

"Yeah."

"Take a smoke break. Before we leave, we have to arrange the net for the next tide."

The net had twisted. We had to straighten it all out. While working, I fell and was now covered with mud. It had dried on my face and I must have appeared like I had a woman's beauty facial. Once we got back into the pickup, Gloria looked over and laughed. "You did good bud."

Dallas Nelson

I had already lived in Dillingham for about seven months when fellow parishioners, the Armstrong family, offered to rent me a white bungalow on the Townsite, a block up the hill from city hall on the same Main Street. There were only about four hundred homes in Dillingham so it was not easy to find one. The large yard was covered with snow. So were the roofs of a storage shed and a steamer. The house included an arctic room, a downstairs bath, tiny kitchen, living room and bedroom. It might have had six hundred feet of living space. There was a steep stairwell leading to the attic which had been equipped as another bedroom with a single window that overlooked Nushagak Bay. The entire place was modestly furnished.

February temperatures were already warmer but still below freezing. Within days, I walked to and from work with metal boot clamp-ons to avoid falling on Main Street which had almost a foot of ice built up. Leaving for home at dusk, Dallas stood on his upper-level landing in a parka, hood up.

"You hungry?"

"I'm always hungry."

"Good. I can't eat all of this caribou filet minion I cooked." He waved me up.

His building was small and home-made, like many in Dillingham. Each floor had about 600 square feet. To access the ground level (where Dallas had his office), one had to use the exterior stairs. Inside the living quarters, Dallas took off his parka to reveal a cook's full-length apron.

"I got carried away. Just lay your parka and stuff on the chair while I get some things out of the oven." He grabbed his oven mittens, put them on. "Did you know Dugan Nielsen grew up in the house you're renting? Even today it's called the Nielsen house." Dallas carefully set a cookie sheet full of caribou steaks on the table. "His dad had the house dragged here on a sled. I brought this building here on a sled too. Downtown rent was too expensive. Now after investing all this money, the city sent me a notice that my building might be affected by a Main Street widening."

He set another cookie pan with baked Brussels sprouts. "These are from the Shilanski garden." He had a third pan with baked potatoes. "Let me get some butter. Do you like sour cream on the potatoes?"

"Butter's fine. Hey! I cleaned all the junk out of the steam anteroom and inspected the steam room. Could you come by and check it out?"

"No problem. Make it Saturday about noon. I have some appointments in the morning. Fritz hurt his back carrying frozen meat up his stairs. Alice hurt her shoulder fighting the Castle fire. Curt says he just hurts."

Dallas put ice in a glass tumbler. Then he poured a generous draught of whiskey. "You want some?"

"A beer would be nice."

He handed me a bottle and we toasted. "May you get your steamer working quickly. Dig in."

"This caribou is really good. Better than beef."

"The locals will tell you if you only ate caribou, you'd die of malnutrition. Have you tasted Shilanski's caribou links? He put some new spice in them and they're great. To hell with nutrition."

"Is the green stuff parsley?"

"Oregano."

Dugan Nielsen advised me to get wooden pallets from the grocery store garbage area. I walked downtown with a length of rope, tied it to a pallet and drug it up the hill repeatedly. Soon there was a stack of them in my backyard. Fritz Johnson loaned me an eighteen-inch chain saw. It was a clear day. First, I pulled nails to avoid messing up Fritz's blade. The stack of pallets became a mound of boards. I had left one pallet intact to use. I laid a board across it. I pulled the cord and got the saw buzzing and started cutting the boards into fifteen-inch lengths. Within minutes, I was perspiring. I took off my jacket.

It took two hours to cut all the wood. My expedition weight long underwear shirt had crept up my back, exposing skin. When I tried to stand, I couldn't. I walked inside like a question mark and called Dallas.

"Yeah, yeah. I'll be there in a few minutes."

He had me lie down and gave me a back massage. Once I pulled my shirt back down, he handed me a jar of stinky cream, "Use this for the next few days. Let's look at this steamer. That's what will really help you."

The anteroom was clean as a whistle. Even the wall mounted hooks were clean. All the dust had been wiped down off the door that led from the anteroom to the steam room. The steamer itself was a room about ten feet wide by eight feet deep. In the center on the floor, there was a bed of stones bordered by clay bricks. On top of the rocks sat a metal fifty-five-gallon barrel. On top of the barrel were large stones held in place by chicken wire. The end facing out had a metal door where wood could be thrown in. On each side were very rustic three row bleachers which I had reinforced. Dallas looked the barrel over, checked the metal door on the barrel, and finally tested the bleachers.

"This will work. Who'd you invite?"

"You, Shilanski, Nielsen and Johnson."

Dallas nodded. "A full house."

"Everyone has meetings. I can take off an hour early to make sure it's cooking by then. Thursday night at seven."

"How's the back?"

"Killin' me and the women at work are constantly teasing the 'old man.'"

Dallas smiled.

At work, I met with the public works director which was hard to do during the winter. They were shorthanded and were responsible to keep all streets and roads cleared. Behind city hall in the dock staging area, they had created a mountain of snow from what they had plowed off the Townsite. The flats, just west of the Townsite, had strategic snow piles as well. That road led to the hospital and the airport. The real difficult zones were the newer areas on the road to Lake Aleknagik, like where the Shilanskis lived. There were frost heaves in Dillingham. You might maneuver your four-wheel drive jeep home in the afternoon and in the morning find a ten-foot-high wall on the road the next morning. Huge pieces of earth would just jut up. Since there was deep snow on all sides, you had to somehow turn around and go home. If you had a snowmobile, you could get to the Townsite that way. If not, you had to wait for city hall to clean up the mess. They brought tractors on trucks and created a detour around the frost heave. Then it took several days to remove it and level the road.

Steve Hardin, the public works director met me in the office. and I asked about a widening of Main Street. "We have a conceptual design, not preliminary engineering or construction documents. They're still trying to find funds."

"Can I see the design?"

"I'll send the plans over as soon as I find them."

By Thursday I still had not seen the plans. I took off early and walked home. I had stashed a pile of newspapers and had a kindling box in the steamer anteroom. I filled a bucket up with water, found a bar of soap and some cloth rags. About the time that I tried lighting the fire, Dallas showed up early. He watched me lighting matches that would not light the paper. He left and came back holding one gallon metal can of gasoline.

"Stand back." He doused the wood and paper, lit a wooden match and threw it in. There was an explosion of flame. When it died down, he closed the metal door with his booted foot. "That's how real men start fires in Alaska."

"Want some baked salmon, canned corn and rice?" I asked.

"Sounds sweet."

We trudged inside and I fed Dallas. He explained, "We have to check on that regularly. If the room heats up to 451 degrees, it will ignite. Most of the fires in Dillingham are due to steamers."

While we talked, Rick Shilanski called. His younger daughter was sick and he'd be late. Dugan called. His wife had a to-do list for him. "Give me an extra half hour."

Fritz Johnson showed up at seven on the dot. We were already stripped down, feeding the fire and sweating. We found a very old thermometer in a corner that still worked. Once Fritz stripped down and opened the door, he found a place on the opposite bleacher.

"How come there's only one bucket?' asked Fritz.

I shrugged my shoulders.

"I guess they don't steam in California," said Dallas. "You're supposed to at least have a plastic bucket, a bar of soap, a scrub brush, a dipper, a cloth for each person," said Dallas.

"I prefer the fiber cloth to really scrub dead skin off," said Fritz.

"And we should have feathers. Where's the newspaper?" said Fritz.

I handed him a sheet. He folded it and fanned himself. "If you have aches or pains, like your back right now, you fan the spot. A feather is better though."

He handed me the paper and I fanned my back. "How hot is it?" I asked Fritz.

"A hundred ten degrees."

"What's a good temperature?"

"Some of the Native Alaskans get it up to one forty."

"Which came first, the chicken or the egg?" asked Fritz. We stared. "The Native Alaskans say they've always steamed. Finns who immigrated here around the turn of the twentieth century already had that custom."

"The Finns also have a native population."

"That's what I mean."

"What about the whale hunters up north? A few years ago, they made a pilgrimage to the Russia and met up with the Siberian natives. They could actually understand each other and had many of the same customs."

We were in there for about a half hour when Dallas jumped up. "I know how to make this interesting." We followed him buck naked through the anteroom and outside. He flopped on his back in the snow and made snow angels.

Fritz did the same. I followed, yelling. That's when my other guests drove up.

We went back inside and sweat more with Dugan and Rick. Since I did not have all the proper utensils, we agreed to use my shower afterwards. At least I had clean towels. Then, we sat around my kitchen table and drank a bit of whiskey. Rick offered me an extra bucket. Fritz promised to give me his extra dipper and Dugan offered me some wash basins he had in his garage and to loan me his eagle feather. The next morning, all my back pain was gone.

The public works director sent me a one sheet conceptual plan without any stamp from a licensed architect, surveyor or civil engineer for the proposed widening of a small section of Main Street, directly in front of Dallas's building. The building encroached upon existing right-of-way by inches. With the widening, this plan showed an encroachment of feet. Since I had done preliminary engineering on roads before, I began to amass official property maps on both sides. Then, very quietly, I began to create a decent base map.

At home the steamer was heated up at least once a week. With their help and some purchases, it was now fully equipped and used regularly. It was very useful on weekends. Seated at the Sea Inn, we drank cinnamon schnaps until most at the table began to head-bob. Dallas gave our secret signal and we snuck out on his snowmobile to steam in an already hot room, then come back sober. Our buddies were falling off their chairs and thought us to be the town's best drinkers.

One night nobody could steam except Dallas. Everyone blabbered about the spring equinox.

"Have you heard the Wood River crack?" asked Dallas as he sat on his snowmobile in my snow-covered drive.

I shook my head.

He handed me a helmet. "Get your winter gear on. We can steam some other night." Dallas had a large Polaris snowmobile that sat two. We headed northeast across tundra under a star filled dark sky. On the banks of the Wood, we parked near the ruins of the Alaska Salmon Company cannery.

"The best time of year for the Northern Lights is spring and fall. You must not have been listening to the radio. There is supposed to be quite the show tonight," said Dallas as he took off his helmet. "Listen!"

We sat silently. There was a low creak, then, another. There was an explosion, like a rifle shot. "What's that?"

"The frozen river. It makes sounds when it cracks. The ice is constantly moving. It's probably several feet thick now. In six or eight weeks, it will begin to melt and break up. That's the most dangerous time. If you were to crash through the ice, underneath that river is moving. It takes you with the current and you will have no chance of getting out."

The light show started. At first the dark sky had brilliant green lines that moved. The lines turned and became wider like a ribbon twisting. They moved and twisted together. It seemed like a cross between a kaleidoscope and a fireworks' display only better. It was hypnotic. Someone once described it as "illuminescent curtains dancing through the night sky."

"There are all sorts of tales about those lights. Locals tell you not to whistle under the Northern Lights because they will descend upon you. It is not supposed to be good. There are also tales of people in the bush who see weird things that appear to happen in front of them but find out later that they happened far away," said Dallas. "Who knows?"

A few days later, I stopped at Dallas's house after work with a six pack of beer. He didn't answer. I knocked again and the door opened fast. Before me stood a Native Alaskan woman wearing an open robe. She only wore underpants. She grabbed at the robe to close it as I stammered, "Is Dallas home?"

"Yeah, yeah. Come in and close the door before my cake falls!" Inside. Dallas was in his large apron, wearing his oven mittens. On the table sat two metal cupcake pans with fresh cupcakes. "This is for Suzie so she has gifts to take home." The woman smiled and moved to the table where she began to spread canned chocolate frosting on the cupcakes. "Close the door! You born in a steamer?"

"Cake doesn't go well with beer." I held up the six pack. "I'll leave this. We can talk tomorrow."

"Suit yourself. This is going to be a good batch. Check this out!" He pulled a chocolate cake from the oven and set it on the counter.

"Dallas is a good cook," said the woman.

The next day I asked about the woman because I did not recognize her. "Oh, she's from a small village. She was here to attend a conference."

"How did you meet her?

"Last year I met her sister. Her sister went home and recommended me."

Aside from my other duties, I started to play with the redesign of the Main Street widening. I found out who did the conceptual design in Anchorage and called him. He gave me all the parameters. This was before the internet and before many of the computerized drafting programs but luckily, I had brought my French curves, mechanical pencils, calculator, and other tools of the trade. Immediately across the street from Dallas's place was an empty lot owned by the Choggiung Corporation, a local business. It was in charge of administering about 3,000,000 acres of land within the Bristol Bay region as a consequence of a 1971 federal law which essentially was a form of reparation. However, instead of recognizing tribes and assigning a sovereign area as a reservation, locals were given shares in a for-profit corporation. It sure seemed like a real estate company/development firm.

This was all new to me. It was almost like learning a foreign language. I was raised in Arizona less than a mile from a Pima reservation and less than twenty miles from an Apache reservation. I knew them both and went to school with Yaqui and Pima. They operated as sovereign nations overseen by the Bureau of Indian Affairs.

Dillingham at that time was an incorporated city with a population almost split by races. A bit more than half were Native Alaskans. Dugan is a Native Alaskan. The rest were non-native immigrants like Rick Shilanski, Fritz Johnson and Dallas Nelson. In order to access federal help, the Native Alaskans had a separate organization called the Bristol Bay Native Corporation. Like Choggiung, it is a for-profit company. Once I had the opportunity of working in their office down the street. Choggiung wanted to open an area for residential lot sale and the BBNC was aiding them by writing the required environmental assessment. When they had a few questions, they called me in to help organize and write.

In late spring, temperatures rose. Ice in rivers and streams cracked, split and they became more akin to giant ice highways. Huge chunks of ice floated at ten miles an hour like a freight train. Likewise, Nushagak Bay's frozen veneer disappeared and once again, you could see choppy waves. Restaurant workers took down plywood from windows. Men and women painted and cleaned as they reopened. The number of flights increased with taxis running non-stop to ferry folks to homes, hotels and a tent city near the dock on the outskirts of the Townsite. At least a dozen locals went to work repairing nets in a warehouse located alongside the dock. Groups of men and women worked on drydock, repairing fishing vessels. As the town awoke, lots of backs got strained. Dallas began appointments at seven in the morning and often worked into the night. For emergencies, he even attended people late at night. The next 100 days accounted for the majority of the town's collective annual income. A resident might walk in leaning on a cane and walk out with it under one arm.

One night while celebrating a birthday at the Sea View with music blaring, Dallas squirmed in his seat, moved his shoulders and arms and made faces as he "danced" to the music. "Would you like to dance?" asked Gloria.

"No, no. I'm too old and tired. I only table dance now. Join me?" And they both squirmed in their seats. Fritz, Rick, Dugan and I all joined in.

I was busy with two technical studies: the road widening and a study about beach erosion along the Nushagak Bay near and along the Townsite. Dugan was working with the Bristol Bay Native Corporation. Fritz and Rick were outfitting fishing vessels and hiring crews. Doctor Dallas was earning his name. I saw many friends and neighbors shuffle into his office before eight in the morning and then saw them skip out at my break time. I had it easy. My only worries were paper cuts and staple punctures.

Halfway through the summer, I completed three alternative widening alignments, none of which would require the removal of Dallas's building. Since I had no idea if any of this might fly, Dallas was unaware that I had been working on it. First, I met with Steve Hardin.

"I have nothing to do with this. If they find the money, it will all be contracted out."

Next, I met with the city manager. "You want to take land away from a Native Alaska corporation to save a ramshackle office? Good luck on that."

Tommy Tilden, our mayor-elect and a Native Alaskan, was much more diplomatic. "You should really meet with the Choggiung C.E.O."

I scheduled a meeting with her at her office. What's her nose was an older lady with a well-furnished, large office. There were lots of framed photos of her shaking hands with politicians. After the perfunctory cup of coffee and small talk, I mentioned the proposed widening. "It will make the sale of the vacant lot easier. I'm researching funding sources now."

I mentioned the expropriation of Dallas's building. "He can relocate." I unrolled the three alternative layouts on her desk. "You did this?" I nodded. "Want a job? You could help subdivide some of our lands."

Our conversation went nowhere. At one point, she raised her voice and got red in the face. It was not that different from the California NIMBY Syndrome: not in my back yard. I set the project down and moved on with others.

Towards the end of the summer, Dallas called me over as I walked home. He was outside, cleaning fresh salmon as we talked. "You been up the Wood River yet?"

I shook my head.

"Fish and Game has an opening coming up for caribou. Shilanski and I are heading up river in his sixteen-foot fiberglass outboard."

"I've never hunted."

"Have you ever fired a rifle?"

"My dad's thirty aught six and an M-16 in the army."

"Perfect! Shilanski's got an AR-15 with a scope. Do you want to go or not? I'll call Rick so that he and you can start target shooting and you'll need the permit. I want more of Rick's spicy caribou sausages."

The very next morning, Dallas herded me to the ranger's office where using my Dillingham library card as identification, I paid five dollars for my in-state resident hunting permit. That same night, Rick picked me up and drove me out of town to our municipal outdoor shooting range. It was a flat area surrounded by dwarf pine trees. There was an old decrepit roof with a splintered counter underneath. One hundred yards away were old stakes. Rick walked down and hung up some targets. After showing me how the scope worked, we began. He adjusted the sight for me. "You need work. Let's come back every night this week." Remember: the sun did not set until eleven thirty and dusk extended until about one in the morning.

Very early on Saturday, I waited at the city dock with my backpack. Following Rick's instructions, I brought my slickers (for mosquitos), my water purifier and my hunting knife. He had already bought some beer, whiskey, food and ice.

"Where's Dallas?"

"He's got appointments. Leon Braswell (a former mayor and bush pilot) will fly him to Portage Creek this afternoon. Hop aboard mate."

The Nushagak and Wood Rivers both empty into the Nushagak Bay. While the Wood drains from the north, the Nushagak drains from the northeast. It was a beautiful clear day with pleasant temperatures. I wore my slickers' overhauls and a t-shirt covered by my long underwear shirt, unzipped and open at the neck. The Nushagak Bay was a bit choppy as Rick gunned the engine. The boat chopped up and down for nearly a half hour. Once Dillingham's look far away, Rick cut the engine.

"Something wrong"?"

"Nah. The belugas will come to greet us."

Within minutes, we could see the back of a large fish near us. "See?"

The fish circled us, coming closer. Soon, he nestled alongside and it's pink back surfaced. "If you jump in, he'll play with you," said Rick.

"Thirty-nine degrees is a bit brisk. No thanks."

"Well, at least pet him."

I tried. The beluga circled, coming closer. Once he surfaced next to me. "Should we feed him?"

Rick laughed aloud. "He has plenty of salmon to munch on."

Rick grabbed a paddle and tapped the water. The Beluga moved. He tapped the water again and the whale moved farther away. Rick restarted the engine and moved away slowly. "We have to be careful not to mangle the fish with our propeller."

Soon, we entered the mouth of the Nushagak. A golden eagle swooped. There was strange splashing all around. "What's goin' on?" I asked Rick.

"They're curious and breach to see us."

I looked closely. They did breach the water. They jumped up in the air and looked at us! I was surprised. Rick cut the engine and baited a pole. He threw it over and had a bite in seconds. Once he pulled it up, he squeezed it to open the mouth. The fish had rows of sharp teeth.

"You have to be very careful with these," he said as he unhooked it and threw it back into the river. "They're also full of bones. They ain't good eatin'."

We passed a bear who clawed fish near a bank. It never even looked at us. Then, we passed a few houses grouped together maybe six feet above the water level, some twenty yards back, surrounded by trees and brush. It was one of the villages whose inhabitants frequented Dillingham. Rick cut the engine.

"Grab a paddle. Let's try to aim for that narrow, deeper part," said Rick. Up ahead, there were sand bars. We paddled like crazy but missed the deeper section and beached. "Damn. I'll take first haul." Rick slipped on waders and jumped onto the bar, grabbed a rope tied to our bow and pulled. Once we were free, he yelled "Get it started and steer to the port."

"Left?"

"Yeah, left."

We chugged. Rick climbed back in. Maybe a half hour later, we beached on another sand bar. Waders on, I jumped down and grabbed the rope, Rick explained, "These bars move by the hour. The river's just coming up. This should be less of a problem as we move."

Once I climbed back in. Rick bid me to sit in front. "If you see a "v" in the water, call it out with "starboard" or "port. The "v" means submerged tree."

We continued up river. "We're headed for Portage Creek which originally was a Yupik overnight summer camp. They portaged their boats on their way to the Kvichak River. In the 1960's it became a settlement. The Bureau of Indian Affairs built a school. The State of Alaska invested as well and a landing strip was built, a tiny dock, an electric plant and the village was wired. Ten years ago, one hundred people lived there. Then, people started to migrate to Dillingham which has more to offer."

We spotted a tiny wooden dock. "Put on those waders. Then, climb onto the bow. When I tell you jump in the water and pull us to shore. Wait for my word."

I was ready as we coasted in slowly. Since we were fighting the current, Rick had to give it some gas, then float, give it gas. "Jump!"

I jumped and sank up to my neck. I could hear Rick swear. He tossed me a rope tied to the bow and I began to walk and pull. Cold water topped the waders. My chest and torso were now very cold. Behind me I heard, "Do you want to get out?"

"No, we're almost there." My boots were now filled with cold water and it was more difficult. I finally helped to beach the boat. We tied it off on a tree. Since the river was rising, Rick did not want to gamble that the boat might slam against the dock. My waders squished as we walked.

Portage Creek was creepy. Officially, six people lived there. Our guide and his family accounted for five. Houses were abandoned like a ghost town. A black puppy squeaked as we climbed wooden stairs. Chris, a tall, bearded, light-skinned man, was in the arctic entry preparing fish bait. A beautiful middle-aged Native American woman stuck her head out of an open door and smiled. Rick gave Chris bear hug.

Chris noticed that I was holding dripping socks. "Someone took a dip." He motioned to his wife, Leona. She grabbed them and put them on a line hanging over the stove.

"You're a bit late. The herd crossed the river three days ago. If you're lucky, we might catch some stragglers."

"How many are in the herd?" I asked.

"Chris looked at me and wrinkled his brow. "I don't know. I never counted them."

"Open your mouth again," said Rick. "Ah ha! You *are* missing a tooth!"

Everyone laughed. Leona held up a pair of plyers and made a twisting motion. "My hometown dentist," said Chris.

The couple had three young children who rarely saw anyone. The excitement of seeing strangers drove them insane. "Look at this!" said the older boy and did cartwheels near the working Franklin stove.

"No, no. Look at this!" said a younger boy and did somersaults on a bear skin. They had a yo-yo so I entertained them with tricks. Leona spooned ground coffee beans into a small fish net. Then lowered it into boiling water in a stove top pan. Rick and Chris checked a map near a window overlooking the river.

"I went out this morning. They crossed here." Chris pointed. "If we were to find stragglers, they'd probably be eating berries here."

Leona handed us each a cup of fresh coffee. "Where's Doctor Dallas?"

"Leon is flying him in. Will that be enough time?" asked Rick.

"Sure. By boat we'll make that valley in thirty minutes, then, we have to hike a mile or so inland."

Chris radioed Dallas at his office. Dallas had more patients than he expected. He would fly in the next day. So, we loaded up.

Within a half an hour Chris shouted, "Beach it there!" We unloaded our rifles and ammo bags. We hiked up and over a hill and into a shallow valley where almost everything had been eaten. There was a pleasant light breeze that blew the mosquitos away. On the ground were stray cloud berried and caribou droppings. I sat down while Rick and Chris followed the herd's trail, then came back.

"Let's load up and head a bit further up river," said Rick.

We moseyed around from here to there for hours before heading down river where a bull moose charged out of the brush and ran down the beach parallel to the boat. The animal was huge! "They run faster than a horse," deadpanned Rick.

"Let's have some fun," said Rick. He made a U-turn. "My guess is that he has a mate in the underbrush, She might stick her head out." Rick gunned the engine near the same spot and the bull moose repeated his charge and run. Rick kept it up until a female moose did stick her head out. It was getting late and we had to set up a camp so we dropped Chris in Portage Creek.

As we headed for our campsite, Rick spotted a single caribou swimming. I pulled out my rifle. Rick reached over and put his open palm on the barrel and pushed down. "It's illegal to shoot a swimming animal. You can fire once it's on the shore."

"I'm going to buzz it. It'll take off running," he yelled as the boat picked up speed. "Do not fire, Larry. Let it run. About fifty yards down the beach, it will stop to look back. That's when you open fire."

Rick grabbed his rifle. "Once it's hit, you jump off for the kill shot. When it goes down, I will be heading for shore. Jump on the bow. When we beach, jump off and lay down the anchor. Then, get on shore with your rifle and give it a head shot if necessary. I'll be right behind you. Take your knife. We want to be fast. The bears will smell the blood."

Rick and I fired simultaneously and the caribou was hit in the front quarter near the shoulder. It went down and Rick gunned the engine, starting his plan. I followed orders. The caribou had a crazed fearful look as it tried to get up and fell. I gave it a head shot, then checked the shoulder wound. It was too clean for an AR-15. Rick's shot brought it down.

Immediately, Rick was at my side. He grabbed two hooves. "Grab the other two, mate." We got it on its back, spread eagle. "I'll gut it. You cut from the neck down to here," he said pointing. "Only use about a quarter of an inch of blade to cut the hide away. Then pull it back a bit." He started cutting while I followed his directions. "That's good. Now push the blade in about a half inch from neck down." He disappeared for a second before I heard behind me, "Use both hands to open the rib cage and scoop out the organs." About the time I opened the rib cage and had my arms and hands inside the animal, Rick appeared with a fireman's ax to lop off the caribou's head. As the ax completed the job, I could feel the animal relax. Rick went back to work on the entrails. "Larry, did you want the antlers?"

"No. I'm not a trophy hunter."

77

Rick went through the organ pile and pulled out the heart and liver. "These are definitely good eatin'. "

Rick appeared at my side with two plastic tarpaulins. He unfolded it. Then, he used a camper saw to split the carcass into two equal pieces. He grabbed one hoof and I the other. We heaved it onto one tarpaulin then back tracked for the other half while Rick wrapped the side and used rope to tie it up.

Cleaning and loading took under five minutes. We left the head and other organs for the bears. "Drive-by hunting," shouted Rick over the droning engine.

We boated further down river to our camp and placed the wrapped carcass in a pit and covered it with some dirt and branches. We set up a large tent and made a fire with mostly wood stolen from a beaver dam. Soon, we cooked some store-bought grub.

Just before dawn, I heard a noise, grabbed my rifle and quietly stepped outside. Rick lay with his rifle pointed towards a mist. I laid down. We both stared at a silhouette was a giant moose. "Don't fire. Let's load up our meat."

Back in Portage Creek we marched to the airstrip. Leon's small plane landed on the cinfer runway. He taxied around and let the propeller idle as Dallas climbed out with his rifle and ammo bag. Leon waved and took off.

"What's his hurry?" asked Rick.

"He has to pick up a sick woman at Clark's Point and fly her to the hospital," responded Dallas. "We just got the radio call."

"Did you hear about the plane crash last week?" asked Chris. Rick nodded. "I was the only responder. The plane crashed right here. Only two of seven survived. A tourist in back had his belt on good and tight. His guts burst and flew all over the cockpit. What a stinky mess."

We did see another straggler swimming. Once it touched the beach, it leaped at least five feet to a knoll above and ran through thick brush as all three of us fired. Rick beached his boat and I jumped off the bow with rifle in hand, running uphill through the brush. Maybe one hundred yards uphill, I found splats of blood on grass. I stopped. Dallas came up, running.

"We must have hit it," I told him.

"The bears will also smell the blood. The bad news is that the bears have a lifetime hunting and we don't. Better head back to the boat," he said.

Only five months later, the city had a funding shortage. This is not unusual anywhere. At a closed-door session, the city council decided to close the library, museum, the planning and recreation departments. This also happens anywhere. About a half dozen of us were out of jobs. I had no hard feelings, having been through this before. I tried my best to say goodbye to all my bush friends and left Dallas for last.

I handed him an envelope and a roll of plans. "This is a special gift."

"What is it?"

"Open the plans first." He did. "These are copies of three alternatives for the road widening that will not require affectation of your building. In government, we're supposed to look for the cheapest options. These are."

Dallas opened the envelope and unfolded an encroachment permit. "Recently I think it was William Darling who wanted to place a guide wire in right-of-way. Nobody in the city knew what an encroachment permit was. We literally had nothing written about it in code nor had they ever issued one before. According to the council, the planning director was the authorized agent to grant such a permit. That, my friend, is an authorization to have your office barely in right-of-way."

"So, what exactly am I supposed to do?"

"Nothing unless someone from the city knocks on your door to warn you of an affectation. Once you close the door, call a good lawyer in Anchorage and fax them a copy of these materials. Chances are very good that the city will agree with one of those less costly alternatives that cause the least amount of damage."

"You're right: that's a hell of a gift."

Bob Petit

His family nickname is "Bubbles" because that's the kind of personality he has: bubbly. We met in the seventh grade where we once competed to see who could write the longest short story. The next year we both played on the same championship basketball team. His Great Uncle Art taught all of us how to play cribbage. One call from Bob ("Art's here. He's sitting in front of the cribbage board.") and we'd be at his place in minutes. In high school, we dated from the same pool of girls, joined the same service club and the boy scouts. Bob and I floated down the Verde River in inflated tire inner-tubes, water skied the Colorado River and camped out on the Puerto Peñasco beach. His father had an old '56 Ford that he donated to Bob's elder brother and him. They had it painted a dark navy blue. When someone rear-ended them, they used white paint on the dented trunk to write "dent ouch" and that became the car's nickname – dent ouch. We were all at his eighteenth birthday party just months before he shipped out for the Vietnam War. Once he got home, he enrolled at the local university where I was now a senior. For one year, we enjoyed an occasional beer together near campus. Once when I needed a place, he put me up on his couch for a few weeks. And he proudly showed me the trailer he and his older brother built from scratch to carry his and his wife's belongings to Anchorage on the unpaved Alcan Highway. They settled outside of Anchorage and raised a family and taught school.

So, it didn't surprise me when he called me early one summer day in isolated Dillingham, Alaska. "Want to fish for salmon near McCarthy and Kennecott?"

"Sure!"

"Jump on a plane this Friday and get your skinny butt to Anchorage. I've got all the gear." Dillingham is in the bush, about 300 miles southwest of Anchorage. It is not connected to any other town by road and the only two ways to access it are by boat (June through September) or plane (it has a runway sufficient for jet airliners).

I already had my state sport fishing license, stamped for king salmon. After nearly a year in Dillingham, I had a pair of rubber gloves used for setnet fishing, a sheathed hunting knife and worn slickers – overalls with suspenders and a hooded jacket made of cotton cloth sprayed with an impermeable plastic. I also had a decent sleeping bag. Alaska is one of the few places in the world where boots, blue denim and long underwear are a fashion statement. We were both dressed like that when he picked me up at the airport early on Friday afternoon.

I handed him a two-pound clear plastic bag of Dillingham smoked salmon. "My neighbor prepared this. It didn't kill his kids so it must be okay."

"I thought maybe you'd learned."

"I've got a shed out back that the town chiropractor and I are going to outfit it for smoking next spring."

We stopped at a small store on our way out of town to buy soda pop, beer, hotdogs, chips – munchies. It was a five and one-half hour drive northeast towards the base of the Wrangell Mountains to an area that had once been used for copper mining. Luckily, dusk began around eleven thirty at night and the stars would not shine until one thirty in the morning. The highway had two paved lanes with a paved emergency shoulder, signs and guard rails. The first thing I noticed on an Alaskan highway was the lack of man's footprints. There were no electric power towers, no far-off electric lit homes, just mountains, trees, creeks rivers and wild life everywhere. Because of their size, it was normal to spot moose and bear. The sky often seemed to cloud up with enormous flocks of birds from all over the world.

The tallest mountain in North America, known as Mount McKinley when Bob and I studied at Yavapai Elementary but now called Denali, was visible from Anchorage about one hundred thirty miles north. Two hours into our drive, we passed it. Everything in the area was green and lush but the mountain was a white mass.

A half hour later, it began to rain. To keep from falling asleep from the rhythmic sounds of the wipers, Bob slipped a tape into his cassette player. He had Creedence Clearwater Revival and we started bellowing. Course, this led to reminiscing about our hometown.

Within another hour, the rain stopped. Bob pulled over. "Pitstop."

"Good idea."

As I started to walk, Bob said, "Piss where you're at, buddy. There's bear."

We did our business. I lit a cigarette and Bob lit a cigar. "I can't smoke in the vehicle. If Carol smells tobacco, I'll get hell."

Except for a car or truck passing every ten minutes, it was quiet. You could hear the wind rustle leaves in trees, birds chirped and whistled. The underbrush rattled as some critter roamed. Looking south, Denali was totally covered in clouds. We popped cans of soft drinks and ate some smoked salmon, just listening.

Driving the paved Edgerton Highway, east, it was trees and more trees. We drove until the there was no highway and Bob veered off on a narrow trail. Tree branches scraped the sides of his sports vehicle. He and his friends had a special place on the Copper River with useful eddies for fishing, Bob explained. Of his three friends, two were brothers and fellow teachers who had already been mentioned in several books for their fishing abilities.

"There's the trucks." Bob pulled up behind two pickups. As we climbed out and stretched, Bob yelled, "Where is everybody?"

"Down here."

We walked through a canopy of underbrush and trees. On the other side, it dropped off steeply to the river. Maybe ten feet below us, his friends sat in fold out chairs next to a fold-out table littered with fish slime and guts and an ice chest. The three sipped beers and toasted us as we climbed down. This river was something like I'd never seen before. It looked like boiling brown stew moving along in front of us at least fifteen miles per hour. Giant trees with roots still attached floated down like a long freight train.

"There're trees underneath the water too," said Bob. "This is a particularly dangerous river with the swiftness and the silt. The river drops quickly in elevation."

I looked closer. The brown water had v's appearing indicating underwater snags. Then, they disappeared as the underwater tree passed. There were whirlpools indicating undertows that appeared and disappeared. This river was swift, deep and treacherous.

"Why not fish at a shallower spot?" I asked as I climbed down.

"Bears love those shallow places and they don't take kindly to city folk interlopers trying to steal their meal."

When we reached the rock ledge where his friends sat, we shook hands and introduced ourselves. Dennis handed me a can of beer, then Bob. This runoff has created an all-out insane river. Reports are that it may calm down a bit by tomorrow."

"We've managed to dipnet ten sockeyes."

"Are you two hungry? Larry, we have steak, hotdogs, eggs, sliced potatoes and salmon," said Dan Reed, Bob's other buddy.

"Hotdogs are quick and easy."

The men had propane stoves and all sorts of cooking utensils. "We eat pretty good on these outings," said Bob and all three laughed.

After our beer, Bob led me back up the cliff, through the brush and trees to the parked pickups. The men already had set up the kitchen. Bob and I cooked up some hotdogs *pronto*. He pulled out bags of condiments and buns.

"My God! You've got everything," I said as we spread mustard on the buns.

Soon, we cleared and cleaned everything, placing all the food in one bag and garbage in another, we tied a rope to it and flung the two bags high into a tree about thirty yards away in case a bear caught its scent. All of us cleaned off the folding table, folded it up and carried it up the cliff as well. It was placed into the pickup bed, the top pulled down and locked. Bob had brought a huge sixteen-foot geodesic tent, a type I had never erected. I followed directions and within a half hour it was up. Under the tree canopy, shadows took over even though it was still light on the cliff and ten at night. We sat around and talked until dark.

We all fit into the tent. Against one wall, a loaded high-powered rifle leaned. Bob explained, "If we have a bear snooping around, we can always try firing a shot into the air. They hate loud noises. It it's tearing open the tent with its claws, shoot to kill."

The sun rose about four hours later. I did not. When my eyes did open, the tent was empty and quiet, no sounds of wind or rain. I pulled on my boots. Bob was walking back and forth along the ledge of the cliff, holding onto a long handle. Several hundred feet way Paul was moving a long handle from an outcropping of large boulders.

"Where's Dennis and Dan?" I asked Bob.

"They're downstream. Want a lesson on dip netting?" He pulled the net out of the water. The plastic pole was ten feet long. On one end was a three-foot wide metal circle with a four-foot deep net attached. "This is an eddy. See how it runs in a circle counter to the river flow and then ends up at the current again? Fish get caught in that too. The idea is to sweep the net counter to the eddy and let the fish get caught, then pull the pole and fish up. Sometimes, the fish lie on the bottom, resting, so don't be afraid to lightly run the net along the silt." Bob lowered it back into the brown turbulent water and gave me a demonstration. Within a minute or two, he pulled it up with flip-flopping -salmon. Bob had a club stuck in his belt. "Use this to pound his head. Then, put him on ice." He opened an ice chest, nearly filled with salmon. Bob had a thick rope tied to a tree up the cliff and attached around his waist. He unhooked it and it ran it around my waist. "Seems a bit thicker than in high school."

"I was a Douglas DC-6. Now I'm a Boeing 747."

"If you fall in, use the rope to pull yourself back out." Then, he handed me the pole and club. "Put on your gloves and get work. I'll unload my inflatable."

It didn't take long before I pulled my first sockeye out. Bob motored by in his sixteen-foot inflatable raft powered by a forty-horsepower engine. He motored over to the cliff where Paul stood. Paul had two ropes. He lowered his ice chest to Bob. Unhooked that rope, then, his. He carefully handed the pole to Bob and climbed down and boarded the inflatable. Next, I heard voices behind me. Dennis and Dan called for my ice chest. "We're close to the limit, Larry. Bring the chest up so we can start cleaning them."

At the camp site, the tent was already down and folded, the kitchen also broken down. They had two folding tables set up with one man at each end, cleaning fish.

Paul showed up with his chest. "Larry! Bob wants to take you for a spin in his inflatable. Just walk down the drive. He's on the left."

Downslope there was a rock-strewn flatter area. Bob had a rope tied to a large rock on shore. "Pick up our anchor, partner. Pull me in so you can board."

Once aboard, Bob handed me a life jacket. "Put this on so we don't get a fine."

I glanced out at the boiling beef stew. "This life jacket won't save me."

"No, it just makes it possible to find your body. If you fell in without it, your boots and pockets would fill with silt within seconds and you'd go straight down. With the jacket, they might find your body stuck somewhere downstream hung up on a tree branch."

Bob caught another salmon, standing up with the pole. While he moved the net, he talked. "When I first came up to Alaska, I signed on to a fishing boat in Naknek. It had a skipper and two of us as crew on the thirty-two-foot wooden boat built in Seattle. Commercial boats cut each other off as they jockey for position. There were some gun shots. This is a lot easier. We basically pulled nets for twenty hours a day which is how I developed Carpal Tunnel Syndrome in both hands."

Back at the campsite, we unloaded more fish and joined the cleaning party.

"Clip the tail like this, Larry. Since this is fish harvest for personal use, we have to identify that by clipping the tails. Otherwise, there's a fine."

"Are you harvesting the eggs?"

"Not today. I didn't bring jars, wire mesh or Procure. We'll dipnet the Kenai later this summer. It's easier and safer."

Mario Ribera Arteaga

Trinidad, Bolivia was still dark when we loaded the supplies into the back of the doctor's jeep. I stopped every so often to double over and grab my stomach as I breathed deep through a cramp. Mario plopped a blue cowboy hat on my head, loaned to me by one of his brothers, he said. It had rained that night but fireflies still illuminated the muddy street. Frogs croaked. The jeep fishtailed down a river of mud for a few hundred yards before Mario stopped to click the wheel hubs into four-wheel drive.

"The sky is too clear," he said as he slammed his door closed and looked up through the mud splattered windshield at the stars. "I hope it doesn't rain more."

Outside of town, we passed a clearing with a neatly cut and crowned road leading to a well-lit, modern concrete building. Mario told me that it was a milk processing plant. "Within an hour," he said, "dozens of men in jeeps will be collecting milk from the surrounding farms and bringing it here."

The highway, a two lane, unmarked strip cut by a bulldozer, ran straight through thick, damp underbrush. The jeep's headlights illuminated cattle, horses, small fur covered creatures which looked like foxes and groups of what I thought were huge hogs. Mario stopped the jeep and told me to get out to look at one. Two walked by the jeep's headlights as I stepped out. They had long snouts and weird skin. Mario told me that they were *capybara*, a South American rodent like a giant four foot long rat that might weigh one hundred pounds! Farther on, Mario had to stop as packs of them crossed the road in front of us. He told me that they slept on the raised highway during flooding, not a good sign.

Mario flipped off his jeep's headlights as the potholed road forked. We entered the tiny hamlet of Casarabe. No more than 500 people lived in simple homes along a sloppy, orange road. Mario stopped in front of one small home where a woman worked on the porch.

"Is Juan home?" he yelled.

"Yes doctor," replied the woman and disappeared inside.

Mario turned to me. "This is one of my cousin's homes. He has eleven children. He raises cattle too," he said before grinning.

His cousin was a tall Bolivian with giant shoulders which made his cowboy shirt shoulders tug. He brushed his long mustache aside and shook our hands firmly. Mario and he talked about family for several minutes which seemed natural enough given its size. Then, Mario mentioned a gas can that he had left months ago.

"Yes, I'll get it," replied his cousin and waved at one of his children to fetch it.

"No, that's all right," said Mario. "I can get it in two days on my way back."

"Room for a passenger on the way back? My son Roberto has an errand to run in Trinidad."

"Sure. We'll be back in two days in the afternoon. How's the road?"

"Bad. I'm not sure you'll make it."

The jeep swayed and yawed as Mario negotiated the river of mud past grazing cattle. My stomach churned. The underbrush was thicker, scraping along the sides of the jeep as Mario whipped the steering wheel from side to side, his jeep fishtailing and throwing up an orange spray that made the cattle scatter. Within an hour and a half, we had traveled ten miles. Mario stopped the jeep at a turnoff where the trees had been hacked back on each side of two wheel ruts. Mario walked ahead to inspect the mud before climbing back in. The jeep's back end broke loose while he whipped the wheel back and forth. Mario explained that he would have to attend to some people in this village before we continued. "There's some incest here. The amount of birth defects is enormous." As the jeep cleared the trees, we raced down a clear straightaway paralleling a creek where children swam naked.

Eviato's children raced naked behind us, waving, screaming and laughing as women dressed in rags cooked in metal pots over campfires. Other women washed clothes by hand in the creek, their only source of water, Mario explained. There were shacks built around an artificial hill. Mario slowed. We passed more wooden shacks with thatched roofs and dirt floors. The only furniture appeared to be hammocks strung from wall to wall.

There was no running potable water, no electricity, no gas. There were no windows and no sign of metal. This was a village from another century. Horses, cattle, dogs and rhea (South American ostriches) ran loose. These thirty families called themselves Siriono and numbered 300.

Our jeep pulled through orange mud, the tires spinning and throwing off clumps as we rocked back and forth. The villagers waved and smiled. They live, as Mario said, "Because God is great and air is free." Mario parked under a grapefruit tree alongside an adobe home which was larger and better constructed than the rest of the village. He pulled up the floor mounted emergency brake, clickety-clack. Mario explained that the local chief or *cacique* lived there with his family. Before we had opened the car doors, children surrounded the jeep, smiling and waving.

"Stick close to me and don't act surprised – no matter what you see," said Mario. Then he smiled and waved at the children as he opened his door.

Mario suggested that one of the boys climb the grapefruit tree. One boy boosted another up and soon, we held four gigantic bright yellow grapefruits which we peeled with pocket knives like oranges and ate while the children formed a tight circle around us and laughed as the juice ran down our chins. Adults walked up slowly, carrying sick children. Mario pulled out a box from the back of the jeep and began tending to deep cuts and handing out medicines. I sat under the grapefruit tree, leaning back to stretch my stomach muscles and breathe deeply through a cramp.

A six-foot tall man wearing clean clothes and boots let the adobe home's screen door slam behind him. He explained that the *llanos* were completely flooded after nearly a week's rain, so we could go no farther by jeep. He offered to loan us two horses. Mario nodded. The *cacique* bid two teenaged boys to round up the horses while we rested. A curious, nearly naked old woman with no teeth stood off to one side, holding a baby. The *cacique* called her grandmother and told Mario that she cared for an abandoned child, fathered by one of Mario's ranch hands.

"I have no food for this creature," yelled the old woman. "Tell him to help me. It is his child and the mother is but a girl."

"I'll talk to him," promised Mario.

Mario had finished healing when the teenaged boys walked over two fine looking small horses which they had saddled for us. A man brought out a chair for me to mount with. I thanked him but mounted cowboy style as the villagers smiled. Mario handed me my backpack. We tied bags down on the rim of the saddles, then rode downhill towards the creek crossing. It was overgrown with trees, and we had to duck branches as the horses strained through the rushing water.

Mario looked back and yelled, "This is the worst part."

The creek was high. My horse lost its footing and almost went down. Unfortunately, the worst was yet to come. Mario waited on the other side, he and his horse enveloped by a swarm of mosquitos. He calmly turned up his shirt collar, pulled down the sides of his cowboy hat and put on a pair of gloves. Our horses climbed onto another outcropping surrounded by thousands of square miles of flooded savannah. This area sat twenty feet higher than the prairie and drained off in tiny rivers. Our horses walked along a path submerged in six inches of water and only partially lit by occasional rays of sunlight that broke through the thick mat of trees and vines overhead. Back home, I had done the reading about Bolivia's geography and had stumbled onto a book by an American named William Denevan. Thanks to his pictures and maps, I knew that this area had once been part of a great civilization, 2,000 years ago. The outcroppings and even islands were built by people known as Mojos. According to Denevan, they created complex earthworks all over north and northeastern Bolivia. They built earthen platforms separated by drainage channels to control not only seasonal flooding, but through evaporation, the ground temperature. But the fields were abandoned, the platforms neglected. Between 1539 and 1569, no less than ten separate Spanish expeditions crossed this area in search of the fabled El Dorado: a place so rich that the inhabitants were rumored to wear gold all over their bodies. They never found El Dorado. Darn fool mistakes are always made by the other dude.

Hordes of blue butterflies followed our horses, sometimes joined by yellow and white ones as if on parade. The forest had all sorts of trees mixed with underbrush. There were hardwoods and even palm trees. Mario kept swiveling his head from side to side, scouting for poisonous snakes and mountain lions. We had brought no weapons. His older brother had told me before we left, "He's nuts! He never takes a weapon."

"Keep looking for lions," said Mario.

"Giddyup!"

"The horse doesn't speak English," yelled Mario and laughed.

"*Adelante*," I shouted at my horse. The good thing about talking to your horse is that he don't talk back.

Soon, we could not hear or see any sign of the village behind us. The forest was silent and smelled humid, a bit rancid. Moss clung to exposed tree roots. The only sounds were the swarming mosquitos, our horse's tails slapping and the suction from their hooves as they pulled out of the six inches of mud to take another step.

It took almost an hour and a half to cover this first tiny part of the trail through the wooded area. Finally, up ahead, we could see where the trees opened and the sunlight flooded through. It was like a huge white door of light. Mario stopped at the end of the tree line and waited for me. In front of us was some twenty miles covered by six foot high grass, occasionally broken by clumps of trees on tiny isolated hills.

The grassland was three feet deep in water. Our path was a river cutting through tall grass.

"Worse than I expected," mumbled Mario. In the dry season, he drove his jeep along this trail.

"*Adelante!*"

We had entered Bolivia's most famous cattle region. This was the Brazilian shield as it might have looked to the Jesuits over 320 years ago. Our horses waded through the flooded trail. The sloshing sounds of our progress echoed off a wall of grass on either side but at least the air smelled fresh. We passed groups of flamingos as we rode. Pheasant and duck swooshed out from the tall grass to take flight as our horses pushed forward. Mario pointed out a minuscule bird's nest in some tall grass above the water line where five tiny birds squeaked.

Then we heard the sounds of rustling grass and water sloshing as if a tank were approaching. The grass was being pushed down by something big. "Cattle," explained Mario. Soon, we were surrounded by a dozen head who upon seeing us stood perfectly still and watched us pass. After we were twenty yards ahead, the sloshing began again. Then again, they appeared ahead of us, waiting. They did that for twenty minutes until Mario took a detour towards a small clump of trees on higher ground. Along the way, we passed a horse's skull. Mario explained that a local rancher's horse had been bitten by a pit viper as they rode through this area two years back. "The horse keeled over dead. The poor man had to walk back carrying his saddle." I searched the flooded grass for snakes and forgot all about my aching stomach. We passed a calf's skeleton embedded in mud. "Must have drowned," said Mario. "The mud bogs can be treacherous."

"Snakes, mud bogs, great," I said aloud and Mario, thinking that I was talking to the horse, reminded me again, "The horse doesn't speak English!"

"*Adelante.*"

We made slow progress until passing a barbed wire fence which led to another, higher wooded area. "This is the University of Beni's land," said Mario. He told me that the

92

citizens of this state had a difficult time creating their first institute of higher learning since the military dictator at that time opposed all universities as "beds of communists." In 1966, despite this, the University of Beni was created. Several years later this property in the wetlands was purchased as a complementary experiment. It was to serve as a test ranch for students. With 4,000 head of cattle, the students began a practicum of their careers: agronomy and veterinary medicine. Here they could test all their book learning and earn some additional bucks for the university through the sale of older stock and bulls. According to Mario, the herd grew to 8,000 head and could have been double that by our visit if it had been administered properly. Problems arose. The herd numbered 1,000 when we rode through.

Back on dry land for the first time in hours, our horses galloped towards a tiny shack. "This was supposed to be a watchman's house," said Mario. "We can rest here for a few minutes."

When I swung one leg up, my foot caught on my rolled equipment tied to the back of the saddle. I leaned forward over the horse's neck to pull my foot loose and lost my balance. Boom! I went down head first to the ground, reins still in hand.

"Thank God you did not do that in Eviato," said Mario. We both laughed as I rubbed the top of my head.

Mario had brought two more grapefruit from Eviato and handed me one. It was sweet and juicy. Mario peeled his slow while looking out at the vast expanse of grasslands. "Such a good idea. Such bad administration..."

We remounted and headed back to our flooded trail, battling mosquitos. They flew into our ears, our noses, our mouths and my fingers swelled at the joints. As our horses sloshed through deeper water, Mario pointed to a strange black cloud moving in our direction. The cloud buzzed like a group of chainsaws. It was a swarm of angry Brazilian bees. Known to attack in groups, they can kill. The cloud was almost funnel shaped and moved erratically towards us at twenty miles an hour, buzzing louder as it whipped one way and then another.

"Just keep riding," said Mario.

"*Adelante.*"

My stomach growled, then cramped into a knot while my backside puckered and I stood up in the saddle, tensing that fat boy up. Mario turned in his saddle and got the wrong idea, repeating, "Just keep riding!" The buzzing was now a roar. Luckily, forty yards behind us, the black funnel skipped off in another direction. I stood again, commanding my backside to listen to reason.

"Just keep riding."

Everywhere we saw birds of all shapes and colors. We even saw a giant South American condor circling and headed in that direction. The condor is just a big vulture that eats dead things, kind of like mortgage bankers. All we found was a soggy fox carcass. We rode on for two hours before reaching more woods. This was the last high ground we would cross for a spell. It was wetter than the last and smelled like a swamp. The mosquitos swarmed and even managed to get into my mountain style sunglasses with leather side panels. As I swatted and tugged at the glasses, trying to rip them off, Mario yelled back, "Just ride."

We reached a barbed wire gate that marked the entrance to another of Mario's cousin's ranch. Mario dismounted. We heard thump, thump, thump and Mario called out.

A skinny sixteen-year-old who was stripped to the waist rode a brahma bull that they called a *buey caballo*. He was a ranch hand at the Suiza, Mario's cousin's place. The ranch hand explained that he had just heard over the radio that his sister in Trinidad had died. He was on his way for prayers and Mass. But the youngster did not trust bulls and did not even want to dismount to close the gate behind him. Mario talked to him for a few minutes before the kid said, "Doctor, could not you take this bull back to Ruben? I'd rather walk."

"To Trinidad?" asked Mario. It was thirty miles over flooded prairie. The youngster nodded. Mario helped him to dismount then stuffed some bills in his hand, just in case he was lucky enough to encounter a bus at the Eviato turn off. The ranch hand bowed and walked off, alone.

Mario tied the bull's lead rope which ran through a nose ring to the back of my saddle. Bulls are afraid of horses. Even this bull, probably larger than my horse, took off running, spooking me, my horse and darn near pulling the saddle off.

"Hit him across the snout with your whip," yelled Mario from behind. I did. The bull slowed and walked behind my horse's rump, then tried to gore the horse in frustration. "Hit him again," said Mario.

The bull must have measured five foot six inches from hoof to top of the back and weighed over 900 pounds. One good swipe of his horns could have torn off my leg. "I don't like this much," I shouted to Mario and whipped the bull.

We emerged from the last remaining trees onto open wetlands. "We're almost there," said Mario. We met two riders, a young man and a teenaged woman. They were Mario's cook and one of his three ranch hands. The young man held his reins in one hand, a rifle in the other.

"I don't like my people leaving the ranch without my permission," said Mario gruffly.

"We won't be coming back," said the young man and rode past us. Mario explained that he had just received his first month's pay and was heading back to Eviato, his home. "He won't do much there except drink and sleep in his hammock until the money is gone, but that's how it is."

Our horses walked steady now on short green grass, climbing a knoll towards a ranch house with a red clay tiled roof shaded by gigantic hardwoods. As we neared a thatched roofed stable, ranch hands waved and yelled. We rode, the bull following close behind my saddle. "Ruben's not the biggest man, but he's tough," said Mario about his cousin.

"Almost from the start, he had a squatter problem and it got ugly. He ran them off though."

At the tiny corral, Mario and I dismounted slowly, painfully. Before I had both feet on the ground, Ruben ran up, talking. The crow's feet next to his eyes tilted up. His cowboy shirt was open, his hair was tousled. He gave Mario an *abrazo* before ordering one of his hands to unsaddle and water our animals. I spotted the outhouse and ran off, lickety split.

Ruben had bought this ranch six years before. He and his wife had sired five children in that time. When I walked to the ranch house, tucking in my shirt, three of his children came out to meet me. They led me to the front porch where a big hammock hung, then pointed inside where Ruben and Mario gabbed about a roundup set for the following week. I snuck back out to the porch and stretched in the hammock, lighting a cigarette and blowing smoke rings as I watched the river flow past the front side of Ruben's house. It had flooded here too. The river was muddy and swollen, ripping past while taking with it trees like a freight train. Submerged snags created v shapes on the surface with swirling, dangerous undertows.

Ruben's wife, a wide shouldered strong looking woman, surprised me as I watched the river. "Lunch is ready. We've been waiting for you."

The dining room was furnished cowboy fashion: one thick wooden table, six wooden chairs with leather backs and bottoms, one cabinet, a revolver and a cartridge belt hung on the wall next to a rifle, hat and chaps. That was it: no pictures and no calendars. Ruben's wife set a plate of sizzling strips of beef down on the table. Mario explained that it was warmed up beef jerky which they called *charke*. A young maid whose bare feet slid along the still damp concrete floor set down bowls of steaming soup and a platter heaped high with wild rice. Next, we were served glasses of fresh squeezed lemonade from a clear glass pitcher which rattled as the ice cubes clinked together.

"The river's risen," Ruben told Mario. "Three days and nights now. You'll have to cross in canoe. Maybe at Antonio's you can mount horses, but not before. I'll go with you."

Everyone was silent as my fork clanked. My mouth opened and my hand grabbed for a glass. Mario told Ruben, "He can't ride so well, but damn, he can eat."

The bowls and platters were all empty when Ruben's wife brought out the coffee pot. Ruben and I smoked and drank. Afterwards, he took the revolver belt off the wall and strapped it on. "This Mario," he said with a grin, gesturing towards my companion with his straw cowboy hat, "He never travels armed. Thinks he can talk a lion or a crocodile out of taking a bite."

We boarded Ruben's twelve-foot-long dugout canoe and began pushing it across the river with long poles while standing. The river had overrun its banks and was a half mile across. My shoulders began to ache. Our canoe snagged on mud bogs more often as we moved towards higher ground. We pushed, grunting and sweating, following the water towards a narrow section leading into shadowed thick trees, underbrush and vines. It was already late afternoon and the birds squawked. Ruben's dugout was very heavy, weighing maybe 200 pounds, but it did not need much water. We went along well for a few minutes then, plunk, it was solid mud. Mario and Ruben jumped over the side and sank up to their waists, moving slowly towards the bow where Ruben said a rope was. They looked at me and I jumped over too, asking if there were not snakes and leeches.

They said, "Sure."

We had no other choice. The mud reached my mid-thigh. My foot sank and even though underwater, when I pulled my leg, I could hear a sucking sound as my boot pulled clear of the bottom. All three of us grabbed the rope tied to the bow and single file, heaved. Course, there were slips. Before long, we were covered with mud and sweating, pulling as a thick mud stew swallowed our legs.

"Leave the canoe," said Ruben. "I'll ride a bull back for it later."

Luckily, we were only 500 yards from Antonio's small camp. First we saw split rail fencing, then two small palm thatched and wall-less shelters. We walked closer. Antonio, tall and muscular with huge shoulders and a wide chest, worked a bull. He waved to Mario and Ruben. From a nearby garden planted in *yuca* and corn came Antonio's wife, a short delicate woman who looked more like a fashion model than a ranch hand's wife.

From a barrel of rain water, I dipped and splashed cool water over my face and chest as Mario and Ruben talked. Antonio invited us to sit down and rest inside one of his thatched roof shelters. He pulled over homemade wooden stools while his wife poured glasses of grapefruit juice. Off in the corner was a homemade long bench with forked sticks rammed into the ground at one end and a thick round shaved trunk set within the forks over the bench. Antonio had built his own bench press. His weights were sacks filled with clay and rock. Maybe Mario was right about my riding, but I knew something about lifting weights. While Ruben and Mario sat quietly, Antonio and I had a serious discussion. First, I lay down on his bench to huff and push, then he. Next, he handed me another homemade weight and we began a bar curl routine. Antonio not only cleared land, broke bulls and horses, branded cattle and built shelters from sunup to sundown, he lifted weights five times a week! No wonder he looked like superman in a cowboy outfit.

He wore me out in short order before we sat back down to drink grapefruit juice while talking about our pilgrimage to Mario's ranch, Michoacan. "Horses won't make it," said Antonio. "The canoe would be difficult. You'd have to carry it over this hill." He pointed up, through the trees, at a mean looking hill that rose a hundred feet. "Better take bulls."

Mario and Ruben nodded. Antonio sent another hand out to round up two bulls while Ruben said goodbye.

"Doctor," he said, "when you come back in two weeks, could you bring me a can of gasoline for my chain saw?"

Mario smiled and shook Ruben's hand. Antonio loaned him a bull that was already saddled and tied to a fence. Ruben mounted cleanly and rode off towards the water.

It began to rain. The drops splashed as they hit the ground. Antonio's helper walked up leading two huge bulls by ropes tied to their nose rings. He tied one to a fence and the other to a pole set in an open area. Antonio got up and held the bull's head cocked to one side and downward as the cowhand saddled it. Their movements were very slow. They repeated over and over in low voices, "So, so, soooo." Once the first bull was saddled, Antonio led him over to a fence and tied him up tight. They saddled the second. They chose the taller and wider bull for me. Antonio pulled its head extra close to the pole and wrapped the rope around several times as Mario and the cowhand stroked its flank saying, "So, so..."

I approached that bull like a porcupine makes love: slow and careful. "Have you ever ridden a bull?" asked Mario as I lifted one foot to mount. They all laughed as I shook my head without speaking. As the bull twitched, the cowhand jumped. Mario and Antonio grabbed, whispering, "So, so..." The darn stirrup must have been three feet off the ground. Even so, I mounted with no problem, but it looked like a long drop as they all let loose. Antonio handed me the rope and a whip.

Mario was another matter. His stomach had been easing over his belt buckle long enough to make the buckle bend and this tended to make it extra difficult to raise his foot three feet off the ground. "I hate riding these damn bulls," he said as Antonio gave him a boost. "They're traitors. Animals throw you, stomp you and run off...Damn rain..." He mounted, then tugged hard on the rope connected to the nose ring. The bull obeyed and turned.

"Now we're even," I told him. "I can't get off and you can't get on."

99

Mario smacked the bull's rump with his whip. "Hee. Hee! Damn bull. Hee!" Hee was Bolivian for giddyup, I reckoned.

My bull did not respond as well as Mario's. It tried to rub me off on a fence post like I was a wad of chewed gum. Antonio came over laughing. "Nobody's ridden this one for a month. Pull hard on the nose ring." He helped guide my bull out to the path at the foot of that hill where Mario waited.

"Hee," I said as mean as I could.

Mario swore under his breath as he pulled on his bull's nose ring. "**Hee! Hee!**"

We cleared the remainder of Antonio's section of the woods and entered the flooded prairie. The rain continued and off on the horizon, darker storm clouds blew towards us. My stomach cramped.

"Now you'll see some crocodiles," said Mario. He meant South American caiman which often reach eighteen feet long. I prayed to the Holy Virgin Mary.

The water got deeper. My bull struggled. As we skirted along wooded area around an especially bad section, the current tugged at my mount and we drifted. It was mighty scary being atop a 900 pound animal drifting in fast running water, knowing that crocodiles could be out there and my buddy was too crazy to carry any weapons because according to his own cousin, he thought he could talk to the animals. Not only that, the brush and scrub trees were just silhouettes against a darkening sky. When the bull finally regained his footing, half under water, meaning that my legs were submerged, he headed for a big dark shadow which probably was a tree: either that or a monster of a crocodile standing on its tail. I lowered my head just before we plowed through branches and I lost Antonio's whip. It might still be floating in the great Oriente of Bolivia. Sorry Antonio.

The air got cool as an evening breeze blew, soaking us with fat raindrops. Partner, a six inch rain in Arizona is one drop every six inches so you can bet that I found this wet savannah tiresome. The only advantage was that the mosquitos all hid. In the dark, Mario told me not to worry about steering. The bulls had visited his ranch before, he explained, and being smarter than horses, they would remember the way. We rode for hours while I massaged my cramping stomach with one hand.

Mario cried out, "This is it! Welcome to Michoacan."

Before us sprawled 6,000 acres: one square mile of flooded prairie bordered by trees. Lightning lit the sky like a camera flash. One good strike anywhere along this trail and we would be French fries, you betchya. The bulls plowed through four feet of water draining off towards Kiara River, an offshoot of the Cocharca. Mario began to shine his flashlight wildly into the surrounding grass like he had lost something.

"Crocodiles usually won't move if you hit them in the eyes with light," he said without laughing.

I whipped out my flashlight and mimicked him. Dozens of pairs of red eyes lit up along the trail all around us. Some of them might have been big. With my legs dangling off the bull in the water, my palms sweat and my mouth got dry. We were fifty-four miles from Trinidad's hospital: fourteen hours by four wheel drive jeep, horse, canoe and bull. Lightning opened the sky and thunder cracked.

"Hee! Hee!"

We entered a definite trail lined on both sides by tall trees which blotted out all moonlight. The only sounds were the sloshing of the bulls and occasional rushing of caiman. Mario's flashlight beam hit another pair of red eyes, then a corral. "This is it." We rode into the corral, dismounted slowly into six inches of mud as the rain splashed in the puddles around us. "I've never see it rain like this," said Mario softly as we untied our bags of supplies.

The corral was built on an outcropping of dirt. Over yonder, two flashlight beams bounced through darkness. I heard the sounds of water. "Alberto and Roberto, good men," said Mario. Mario had only bought this ranch nine months before my visit and his men had already built three camps. Mario was in the process of building his herd from 200 to 1,000. Mario explained that this camp was surrounded by two acres of felled trees and fence. A stilted wooden A-frame shelter without walls stood on another tiny rise twenty yards from the swollen river. While the hands unsaddled our bulls, we waded through water sometimes waist high waving our flashlights in all directions.

Mario had hoped we would arrive early in the afternoon. He said that crocodile hunting at night from canoe was real fun. My lower back hurt from the horseback ride, my shoulders from the canoe and my upper back and arms from tugging on the bull's nose ring. We both had saddle sores, mosquito bites, were covered with ticks and wet. It was also seven o'clock at night. Neither of us talked about fun.

Under his thatched roof, we sat down at a simple wooden table to eat. One of the hands brought out a hot metal plate filled with *charke* while the other filled metal bowls in front of us with a brown meal. He then added cold water. "It's called *chive*," said Mario. "It's made of *yuca*."

I ate one spoon full after another, each more bitter. Mario watched my lips purse and laughed, then told me to eat it with *charke*. Partner, I've tasted better yellow snow. I pushed my bowl away and said, "This is the worst food I've ever tasted." The ranch hands stood perfectly still, then burst out laughing. Mario looked at me and laughed too just before he handed me a stale butter roll, pushed the plate of hot *charke* towards me, saying that I could make a sandwich. They knew that the best seasoning for range cooking is a salty sense of humor.

My bed was two split logs which held several rough cut planks just above the dirt. Roberto hung a mosquito net for me as Mario gave last minute instructions to Alberto. The river splashed only thirty yards away. I wondered if the caiman could smell the *charke* on my breath.

When my eyes opened again, it was light, but still raining. Mario was already drinking his coffee and ordering the hands. I took my mosquito net down and folded it. The river was now ten yards from our shelter. Raindrops splashed all around. The sky was an ominous grey with no strong streaks of hopeful light. Just then, mosquito net in hand, my backside did the twist, then puckered so loud that even Mario heard it smack.

"We would better leave early," he said. "The water's still rising. We stay here and we might be stuck for a month until the river goes back down."

The river did not interest me none, but an outhouse did. Where was it? Mario pointed one way, then another, then a third. "Anywhere," he said while I stuffed my fat feet into boots and slipped and slid out. One cowhand elbowed the other. My pants dropped right there, me hunched over while standing until I heard some splashing. Now I'm hunched over while standing over yonder until I saw a tail. I moved fast while Mario's men cackled. Lucky for me that the caiman had never have seen a backside as big as mine and it scared them all off.

Mario fed me *charke*, rolls and hot coffee before we resaddled our bulls and headed out. A quarter of a mile from camp, we heard loud splashing behind us. Two of Mario's horses were following us. "I'd better take them back," he said. "They'll only follow to deep water and Roberto could spend a week searching for them. You go on."

Mario forgot that I had only traveled this way once, at night. I did not remind him. He rode off in one direction while I trusted my bull to know the way. Many a thing a man does is judged right or wrong according to the time and the place. Forty minutes later, the bull had taken me to a faraway knoll to graze. I turned him around and backtracked to a fork in the flooded trail that was now a river. The water had risen another half foot during the night. It could have been our trail or just another trail. The bull plodded along, splashing as I head bobbed, looking for caiman.

Behind us, I heard that familiar splashing sound coming up just as my bull entered a bend in the flooded trail. We waded through deep water, the bull's back began to buck up and down confusing me. Who has ever ridden a swimming bull? I did not know that when a bull swims, the rider should jump off, reigns in hand and swim alongside or grab onto the tail. With a rider on top, a bull can drown. Mr. Tenderfoot, yours truly, grabbed tight around the bull's neck. Drowning may be a cure for bad habits, but gosh darn, with caiman as lifeguards, Confession sounded a might easier.

"It's swimming!" I yelled to Mario somewhere behind me, still out of sight.

Lucky for both of us, the saddle loosened and twisted to one side, throwing me into six feet of running water. My wet head swiveled as I looked for caiman, still holding onto the rope as if it were a weapon. We raced along for ten yards, I was in the lead, then he before touching solid ground. Well, we both struggled up in the mud. The bull rocked back and forth from side to side, trying to get footing, scaring me worse than a girlfriend's father cleaning his thirty-eight during dinner. Bolivia is no place for amateurs.

But the bull did not fall. I waded towards a tree, rope in hand, to tie him up before readjusting the saddle. Mario's beast came splashing through the water as Mario wisely guided him along the shallower edge.

"You did not let go of the rope!" exclaimed Mario. "Good. He would have kept going without you and it's a long walk."

At Antonio's we left the two bulls and reboarded the canoe which Ruben had left behind for us. With all the rain, the river had risen and our dugout glided smoothly. We found Ruben seated on his front porch, working leather. We told him our story of the swimming contest as he rocked back and forth, laughing. His wife brought out grapefruit juice as we all discussed our return to Trinidad. Mario and I had ridden horses from Eviato. He had asked Ruben to graze one and to loan us another. There was not any other to loan us, said Ruben. He turned and ordered one of his hands to saddle a horse and a bull. I pulled a coin from my pocket and offered to flip Mario for the horse, but he volunteered to ride the bull. There are the moments when one really appreciates the Catholic notion of guilt.

After lunch, we mounted but Mario's bull would not move. "Bulls are afraid of horses," he reminded me. "Ride up on his flank."

I obeyed. This was the first bull I'd ever seen run that fast. All through the wooded area surrounding Ruben's ranch, my horse rode the bull's flank, then through the flooded prairie, my horse weaving from one flank to the other while I yelled to Mario's bull, "Hee! Hee!" and Mario cackled madly as he bounced up and down.

Riding through the university land we slowed. Mario's bull was sweating. Mario pointed to some wooded hills off in the distance. "All that land is owned by a crazy old man who once put together the most successful and crooked ranch in these parts."

According to Mario, the old man had started with 6,000 acres and some cattle. As he enlarged his herd and hired more hands, strange days passed. Cattle from surrounding ranches gravitated through his fences and were mysteriously rebranded. Just before payday, ranch hands took off without telling anyone. The old man got richer. He grew sugar cane. Then distilled his own rot gut liquor which he bottled in a famous brand name bottle. It was later sold locally as if it were the famous brand. Next, he grew tobacco and mixed it with chopped newsprint. They were rolled and sold under the name of *cigarros de allá*, cigarettes from there.

His herd numbered over 8,000 when things fell apart. One wife after another deserted him. His sons left. He grew old. That's about when Mario bought some cattle from him. Mario said that the old man's home was falling apart as was the old man's memory. So much so that after Mario bought the cattle, the old man sent a threatening note demanding payment.

"I'd already paid," said Mario. "So, I rode out personally to show him the bill of sale. That was the end of it."

Even on the open prairie, the water had risen considerable. Mario decided to take a detour through slightly higher ground. There was no trail. My horse sloshed through the water, plowing down the six-foot high grass. Ticks jumped. Ducks flew. My stirrups acted like magnets collecting iron shavings as we rode. Soon, they dragged more grass than a California hippie-dippie on his way to a rock festival. Suddenly, my horse's head jerked down to one side as if he were about to fall. I reigned him in. Mario turned around.

"Did you see a snake?" he asked.

"No."

We continued, Mario looking behind to check our progress like mother duck keeping an eye on the youngins. The bridle hung funny to one side and reaching down, I found a loose end. The horse had caught it on grass and ripped the leather when I reined him in. Thank God his mouth was not cut by the bit. My boots sunk to the ankles as I dismounted and tied the loose ends together. Mario nodded and smiled.

Our progress was further slowed by mud bogs. Twice my horse got stuck, chest high. The second time, I jumped off just as he was going down, I one way and he the other. Course, I was immediately cemented waist deep in brown sticky mud. Mario, not noticing, commanded his bull to pull the horse out. The horse whinnied and flayed its legs as Mario's bull dragged it forward, almost toppling on me. My horse and I were both covered in brown with grass stringers here and there. My hands, face and neck were a mass of red bumps from yesterday's mosquitos, my teeth still sported clumps of half-eaten beef jerky.

The rain stopped. The sun shone over the top of the last wooded section surrounding the ancient man-made refuge, Eviato. The creek gurgled. As we dismounted, children ran over. They were followed by adults. The old toothless woman hobbled while carrying Mario's ranch hand's illegitimate child.

"And the food?"

"It's all settled, grandmother," said Mario. "I'll bring food on the next trip."

Mario attended the children until late that afternoon. I sucked grapefruit under the shade of a tree. My stomach had calmed which according to Mario was thanks to the *chive*. He cured a child with a crushed finger nail, another with a deep cut on the sole of his foot and a third who suffered from dysentery. Once finished, we climbed into the jeep slow, moaning and complaining of saddle sores.

"I was hoping you'd get to see a mountain lion," said Mario as the engine turned over. "They're impressive."

The jeep fishtailed through mud, throwing a shower of orange on the naked children who chased us, laughing. Trinidad was only five more hours away.

Herb Schmidt

He knocked on the wooden door jamb of our open double kitchen doors, smiling as we slurped soup. Herb claimed that the Peace Corps Director had sent him, knowing that we would get along. Jeff and I waved him in, gave him a seat at our wooden unfinished table and served him some soup and a beer. We listened some more, a bit suspicious, having recently dealt with strangers who over-stayed their welcome. Well, Herb assured us that he was going to organize a whiz-bang fishing cooperative and that Honduran fishermen would build him a hut in no time. We knew two other volunteers who worked with the fishing cooperative: it was not known for hard work.

We sat in our tiny, humid kitchen with the wooden doors and shutters open to catch a light afternoon breeze that blew wisps of dust in from the clay street out front. We lightly brushed away flies with one hand and drank beer from sweating bottles with the other while Herb told us stories about life in Belize where he had just spent three years as a Peace Corps volunteer accountant. He had a tortoise shell bracelet, strange feathers and other exotic trinkets. Jeff glanced quickly across our table, smiled and nodded. When we finally opened a walk-in pantry whose door led to the kitchen, Herb threw his pack in and set his guitar against a wall. The room was tiny: maybe five by seven feet. It had one barred window and some wall-mounted shelves on one end. We figured that it had been built as a pantry or a maid's room. The Peace Corps did not pay us enough for a maid or extra food.

"Perfect. What's my share of rent?"

How much is fair for room that would be a walk-in closet stateside? Jeff and I had to think about that for a few days. We told Herb to stay for free until the end of the month to see how much progress the fishermen made on his hut. Within days Herb bought a mattress. The door would not open until Herb stood, set the mattress on its side along one wall. Together with the barred windows, this seemed like a real hazard in case of fire.

"I won't smoke in bed."

Soon, he began to contribute twenty dollars a month for rent. We rotated dishwashing and cooking chores. Aside from full use of the house, Jeff granted him use of his patio hammock six days a week. Jeff and Sandy used it on Saturday nights. They said it was very erotic.

Herb seemed to have lots of time. We found him playing his guitar in the kitchen many afternoons. Since I liked to sing, but had lost the high notes, he learned some Neil Diamond songs. A few times, I caught Herb reading a Denver newspaper, turned to the stock market section. Just before entering the Peace Corps, he had begun to play the penny stock market. Beginning with one hundred dollars, if I remember correctly, he had begun to play the stock market, researching and changing investments. When we met three years later, he had worked his investment up to five thousand dollars. For Herb, it was gambling. Well, Jeff loved poker and the ponies so we all had something in common: I liked music, Jeff liked gambling and Herb liked both.

While it was true that we always treated visiting volunteers to beer at the Big Bamboo (a sailor bar), food at Maxims (with the best conch soup on the Caribbean North Coast) and dancing at Ginette's Hall (a wild and woolly bar for Black dock workers and local women), the really great places were secret. We quickly included Herb in on all our secrets. We knew on which corner to buy the most *deliciosa pupusa*, which vendor had the spiciest *salsita* to put on those *taquitos*, which corner *trucha* would sell us *aguardiente* any time if we knocked right, which bars were quietly romantic, which places had the most sailors (who loved to buy drinks for other foreigners). Most importantly, we knew where the best music was. You could hear Freddy Fender singing all over town but the Big Bamboo had Elvis. Ginette's Hall had reggae and rhythm and blues. A tiny place in the downtown had the Blue Danube Waltz. Delva's father, an Afro-American ex-pat bar owner, had the Detroit Motown sound.

If you wanted songs in Spanish, it was the pool hall around the corner from Ginette's Hall.

Herb loved practical jokes. Once a week, he and I went to the tiny bar/restaurant with the Blue Danube Waltz on the jukebox. Sometimes I treated, sometimes he did and sometimes we went Dutch treat. One evening, near the end of the month when the pantry and cooler were bare and our wallets light, he insisted that we go. We agreed to have one beer, Dutch treat. Hey, call me crazy but when you are thousands of miles from home, surrounded by people who speak a strange tongue, a familiar song is much better than drugs.

As we pushed the western styled louvered swinging doors open, the waitress pulled a coin from the front pocket of her apron, plunked it into the jukebox and hit our favorite number. We smiled, most naturally.

Once we had drunk our beer and heard the Blue Danube Waltz three times, Herb ordered another round with the wave of his hand and a smile. While I tried to wave her off, Herb flashed a small roll of bills. Then, he stood, hitched up his blue denim pants and walked to the bathroom.

After he came back, we drank our beers. Herb slamming down his bottle on the table and everyone looked over, Then, in one swift motion he slipped off the chair and ran out. The doors were swinging before I could speak. The owner, the waitress and two men with thick wrists (like fishermen) looked at me. I had enough money for one beer but we had drunk four. The owner twisted his mouth and narrowed his eyes as the waitress repeated my story to him: that my friend was only playing a joke on me and that I could pay him in ten days when the United States government paid me. He whispered something to one of the men just as I jumped up and made for the swinging doors. Herb was standing on the other side, back to the wall, laughing.

Another evening, Jeff, Herb and I went to the Big Bamboo which was filled with German sailors having a great time speaking German to the owner, Egan, an ex-merchant marine. The jukebox was lit and playing Elvis at full volume as we sat down, waving to Egan's girlfriend. Egan was stooped over, joking with a group of huge men with wide backs, thick necks and arms like rugby players.

Once we toasted our amber colored beer bottles, Herb shouted something in German, then looked up at the ceiling as if he had said nothing. My hair was cut short like a German. My light-colored hair and blue eyes looked German. That night I wore a light turtle neck like a sailor might. Worst of all, my maternal great grandparents were German immigrants and some say I kind of looked like them.

So, the bar-room German sailors all turned around and looked directly at me. The biggest one with tattoos on his forearm and an ugly scar on one cheek, smiled. He was missing his front teeth. He walked over to our table, laid a thick hand down and lowered his head, speaking German with his nose almost touching mine.

"*Nein. No specken de Deutsch,*" I said.

He continued to speak low in German without smiling.

"*No hablo Aleman,*" I said. He squinted. "I'm an American. I don't speak German."

"Amerikan?" He turned to his friends and said something in German. Everyone laughed including Egan the owner. The sailor slapped my back, "But you **look** German, yah?

Egan's girlfriend brought us another round and explained that the German sailors were setting us up all night. We looked over, the group held glasses high and we reciprocated. "What the hell did you yell, Herb?"

"Fuck your mother. It's the only German I could remember."

Once my work in La Ceiba was complete, the Peace Corps reassigned me to the capital. Herb and Jeff came to visit a few times. On one trip they explained how they spent a night in jail after I left. According to Jeff, while drinking in the Big Bamboo they had a tiff, made up and as they stopped in the alley to relieve themselves, soldiers with rifles marched them to the hoosegow since Hondurans do not like

111

weenie-wavers. Herb remembered it differently. He said that while arguing in the Big Bamboo, Jeff told Herb to kiss his hairy ass. Herb told him to climb on the top of the table and drop his pants. Jeff did. Herb did. Shortly thereafter, according to Herb, soldiers carrying rifles came inside the bar to march them off to the hoosegow. Hondurans are not kiss-ass types.

Both agreed that they were lucky that another volunteer had been arrested with them and placed in the same basement cell with a barred window. From the open window, they could see passerby's ankles and yell. They got a kid's attention and convinced him to contact the other volunteer's Honduran wife. If the Peace Corps found out first, it might have been expulsion. His Honduran wife knew how to pay a bribe and they were released. To my knowledge, Herb never kissed another ass in public nor did Jeff ever admit to weenie waving.

I was the first to leave, bound for Mexico City. Within a year, Herb and another female Peace Corps Volunteer friend showed up. They had been in Costa Rica and then Nicaragua during the counter-revolution. First, Herb had taken to sleeping under his bed to avoid nightly machine gunfire that splintered his wooden shutters. Later, when someone was hung outside his front door from a light post, he decided it was time to go home. Chris, our mutual friend, was also ready for home. In fact, they would continue north the very next morning, on a shoe string. I put them up and noticed that Herb was taking some sort of pill. He mentioned that he was sick but that it was not serious. Chris glanced at him. Her eyes moistened and her bottom lip quivered.

Months later, Jeff and Sandy came through Mexico City. They explained that Herb was very sick and had returned to Colorado, his home state. Two years later, Jeff, Sandy, Maggie-Rita and I found each other, all living in the Bay Area. By coincidence, Herb was visiting and we arranged a reunion at our apartment. I had been experimenting with hypnosis and put on a parlor demonstration. Herb had just finished massage school and was now a licensed masseur. He gave me a great massage on the living room floor where we all talked to late into the evening but not about Herb's illness.

We were not sure exactly where he was or what he was doing until one day I found Herb seated behind the steering wheel of a red convertible 1964 Plymouth Valiant that he had borrowed from another friend. The car had been restored and looked and felt like new. We drove over the San Bruno Mountains, a breeze blowing our hair, to Pacifica where we walked the pier eating popcorn and talking. That was the first time that he explained that he had leukemia.

"When the Peace Corps released me after five years of service, my idea was to see South America," he said. "I bused through Nicaragua and Costa Rica. In Panama City one night, I collapsed and woke up a day later dressed in olive pajamas in a hospital."

"Mr. Schmidt," said the doctor, "you have leukemia and we believe that you only have days to live. We cannot release you onto the streets but have notified the embassy so that they can get in touch with your next of kin."

Herb made friends everywhere. Within days, he had accumulated enough sheets to make a rope and that night, jimmied the second-floor window open, threw the rope out and began to rappel down. The rope was too short and he jumped, almost breaking an ankle before limping off into the darkness still dressed in pajamas. The next day, dirty from sleeping outside, he limped into the U.S. Embassy to identify himself and request assistance. They threw him out! He begged in the streets to survive and went back two days later. By that time, his mother and brother had been attempting to contact the American Ambassador in Panama.

"Mr. Schmidt! Of course, right this way," said a marine. This time around, they helped Herb get cleaned up and dressed before boarding a plane to Denver. Luckily, his brother was a medical doctor and was already investigating how they might be able to help.

Herb didn't care for death banging on his door. He tried all sorts of experimental drugs and even operations before heading for South America where he hoboed across Colombia, Ecuador, Peru, Brazil and even large swathes of Argentina. His friend with the red Plymouth was a wine distributor. Together they traveled to North Africa, France, New Zealand and back to Argentina before trying Brazilian wine. Herb liked it so much he stayed a few months, learning a bit of Portuguese.

His trips to the Bay Area became more frequent. "The best national park systems in the world are in New Zealand and Argentina," he told me. Each trip was unexpected and welcome because you just never knew where the heck Herb had run to. Once he showed up practicing Tai Chi since he just returned from Hong Kong. He used Tai Chi as a sort of alternative medicine, quit smoking and seldom drank alcohol. He traveled to China to buy anti-cancer green tea.

Herb's finances had been a mystery. Then on one visit, he explained that since the Peace Corps had not detected his condition, before, during or after service (five years), they had agreed to pay him a monthly stipend. He worked too. I remember one particularly cold, overcast California winter when Herb showed up fit and tan after spending the summer building homes for someone he met in a bar. You never knew what to expect from Herb.

Even after he quit smoking, Herb never lost the habit of grabbing the tip of his tongue with his thumb and index finger as if he were taking loose tobacco from his mouth. He also had a sly grin after telling a pun. In the later years, his pranks disappeared.

The next time we saw Herb, he announced that he had changed bands and gone gay. "My odds for finding a Friday night date just doubled," he explained. I never had met anyone who decides to be gay after the age of forty! But hey, with Herb... He was still our friend and he invited us to meet some of his new San Francisco friends who worked in the live porno shows. It was a folkloric experience.

114

My wife was very pregnant when Herb came again in the loaned red convertible. He and I drove to Half Moon Bay for a sandwich. We spotted a group of sea lions sun bathing on rocks near the shore, so we joined them. Surf spray tickled as it splashed on my bare chest. The combination of the surf slamming and splashing and sea lions growling at one another made it hard to hear everything Herb said. He was tiring of the race with death.

My first-born son was already crawling when I found the red convertible parked in my spot. I pulled in right behind it. A man seated on the passenger side turned to stare but did not say a word, so I climbed the outside stairs up. Inside, Herb was tickling Zeke on the sofa. Herb explained that he just finished a conference on death and dying and was on his way to the airport. The man in car was an acquaintance who had also attended. "He has A.I.D.S.," explained Herb.

By then, we knew that this disease was not transmitted through the air. I went downstairs. Bending down near the car window, introduced myself and tried to convince Herb's companion to come up for something to eat and drink. He smiled but demurred.

Herb smoked for the first time in years. He also drank a glass of wine while describing his adventures at the conference. Standing near my kitchen window, his neck, face and arms looked yellow and I mentioned this. Herb half-turned so that my wife could not see and pulled up his shirt. His stomach was swollen and horribly twisted. His spleen did not work anymore. It was scheduled for removal in a few days. When it comes to anatomy and medical science, I am a dunce, so I asked Herb what that meant.

"The spleen filters out poisons."

My wife remembers this last visit clearly. She thought that she recognized a bit of regret as Herb played with my son. We spent a half an hour talking about adventures and telling jokes, Herb grabbing his tongue for a split second between his thumb and index finger.

His sprint ended shortly after that, more than a decade after it had begun.

Rick Shilanski

"What's your plan for Christmas Eve?" City Councilman Rick Shilanski asked me while seated at Dimitri's counter. It was filled. Plates rattled, the cook yelled out orders, all around us, locals talked.

At that moment, Dimitri himself placed my plate down in front of me with the usual: two eggs over easy, four links of caribou sausage and toasted wheat bread. "Breakfast of Champions," he said, leaning forward and raising his voice. "Enjoy."

I nodded at smiling Dimitri. "I was going to wash and dry some clothes but it's not an emergency. What's up?"

"Why not come to my place? It will be me, the wife and daughters. We have plenty of food. No turkey, just an Alaskan meal."

I arrived about noon during a light flurry of snow. The sun would shine for about four more hours. The Shilanskis lived out of town in a typical 5,000 square foot Alaskan home with balloon style construction filled with extra insulation, pitched roof covered with shingles. Rick had built several small structures on the two-acre lot, two garages, one for snowmobiles and boats and a tiny one room butcher shop with wall-mounted cabinets, long work tables and a chain hoist with stud hanging metal hooks. He had wired it for electricity and hooked up well water to a large utility style sink. Originally when he arrived in Dillingham, years before, he worked as a butcher out of a tiny run-down shack in the Town Site. Later, the giant man was recruited for salmon fishing. Later still, he won the admiration of a boat and permit holder who hired him as a boat captain. That was before the accident.

Nobody answered the side door bell but the door was open. I ambled into their Arctic room: an unheated fifteen by twenty-foot room with benches on each side and hooks on the walls to store cold weather gear before actually entering the house. I stripped off my pea cap, arctic gloves, parka, wool sweater, wool Canadian leggings and cold weather leather boots.

"Hello?" I asked as I walked into a kitchen area.

His wife Janice was working at a stove, perspiring. "Oh! You found your way in!" She wiped her hands on an apron and did a double-handed shake. "Rick! Larry's arrived. Rick!"

I felt a light bump on one leg and looked down. A little girl seated in a low-riding plastic tricycle had run into me. "I'm seven years old," she said.

"Aria, this is Larry. He works with your father."

"Do you fish?"

Janice came and pushed the tricycle down the hall a ways. "You're not supposed to ride in the kitchen. Kelsa! A little help here!"

Rick appeared. "Tour?"

The dining room and living room was a huge open area of maybe 600 square feet with a thirty foot high ceiling of exposed, varnished logs. Facing everything was an enormous picture window through which you could see pines. While the older sister tried to keep the younger sister from pestering me, Janice kept stirring and pulling rolls out of the oven. "Rick! We need a few more minutes! Show him the pool hall."

Rick had one large room with a professional pool table in the middle, pool cues in racks on each wall. Soon, we were shooting pool. Rick had all winter to practice and he was good, even showing me trick shots. The pool room was his, with photos on the walls of his thirty-two foot long fishing boat, shots of crew members pulling on nets, repairing nets, even of other boats. He pointed to one photo of a group of boats.

"That was just before fish and game announced an opening. If you look close, here," he said and pointed. "There's a man holding a shotgun in the air as a warning. It can get hairy out there. This is everyone's ninety days to earn a year's wages."

He explained how the price of salmon was high in the late 1980's but had been dropping since. It was harder and harder to make it. "The Russians were the first non-natives in this area. They showed up in the early 1800s and built a trading fort and a Christian mission. Two generations later, the States bought Alaska and built a weather station inside the fort. The remnants of the fort are across the bay on those flats. Archaeologists have been digging for some time."

A generation after that, an exploratory mission cited the confluence of the Nushagak and Wood Rivers as a great place to harvest salmon as they migrated upstream during the summer. By the beginning of the twentieth century, ten canneries were built to supplement the fishing. When I arrived at the end of the century (1993), there were two operating canneries, a municipal water purifier, an electric plant, an airport with a runway long enough for large jets, a post office, a volunteer fire department, a small police force, a junior college, grammar school, high school, a local radio station, two grocery stores, a few restaurants, a hardware store, two cantinas and eleven churches, as well as other small businesses like a small press (Mosquito Press). There were also seasonal businesses which began to reopen every year at the end of May and closed back down by the beginning of September. During the winter there were about 2,200 inhabitants which increased to more than 6,000 during the salmon season starting in June. Dillingham was considered a regional commercial center.

"Some scientists believe that the Dillingham area has been home to Native Alaskans for more than 2,000 years, fishing and hunting. The Native Alaskans have a long history of sun drying salmon strips, like salmon jerky. It's tasty."

Rick's older daughter stuck her head in the room, "Time to eat."

As we walked down the hall, his wife called out, "Rick, Larry! I need some help carrying platters." And so she did. There was a huge platter with Alaskan crab legs, cut in half and steamed. Each half was about three feet long. There was a platter of Alaskan lobster tails, also steamed. Finally, there was a two-foot-long rainbow trout garnished with orange slices. She had placed baked potatoes, cooked broccoli and sliced cooked carrots in separate bowls. The food filled Rick's giant wooden table.

We sat down and Janice took my hand as everyone took someone else's hand on each side. Rick said, "Thank you Lord for these delicious Alaskan fruits of our labor and thank you for the presence of our new friend, Larry." Everyone said "Amen."

"Larry! You want the fish eyes?"

"I pass."

"I'll take them," said his youngest daughter.

"Larry! You wanna try crab legs?"

"Sure. How do you eat them?"

Janice grabbed one in one hand and a nut cracker in the other. She crushed it a bit. "Just crack it and suck. Use your hands but you need to try a piece of the trout too."

"All the vegetables come from either our garden or my sister-in-law next door. We work together on planting and then barter the harvest," explained Rick.

Eventually, we talked about the San Francisco Bay Area where I had come from which led to our conversation about their last port of call. His wife was from back east while Rick was from Texas where he had some problems before scampering off to Alaska and a new life. Just a few years before, he was crushed by a salmon fishing boat.

"The doctors didn't think he'd make it, let alone walk again," said Janice.

Rick changed the subject. "A few years before that, I flew my mom and step-dad up. We took them on a picnic along the shores of the Nushagak River. My mom carried her pet chihuahua everywhere. While we were laying out the blankets and unloading food, she set him down. Then, we heard the dog yelping but it was nowhere to be seen. Off in the distance on a rise, I spotted the dog being torn apart by a golden eagle. Apparently, it had swooped down when we were all distracted. There was nothing we could do. We're all part of the food chain here."

We barely finished the main course when Janice brought out a hot cloud berry pie and strong coffee. Just weeks before, another Dillingham friend had invited me to pick wild berries with him just out of town. He parked his four-wheel drive jeep just off the road. From the back, we grabbed buckets and then he handed me a high-powered rifle.

"Do we have to shoot the berries before pickin'?" I asked.

"No. You shoot the Grizzley bears if they charge. They also like berries."

"Best target?"

"There won't be much time. Open mouth and/or nostril. A skull shot will bounce off."

We were all helping to clear the table when Janice asked, "Have you ever seen the Snake River?"

"No."

"Ever ridden a snowmobile?" When I shook my head, she told Rick. "I can clean this all up, Get 'em out of the shed."

Outside, the clouds had cleared, the snow flurry had stopped and the temperature had dropped considerably to well below freezing. Rick had two snowmobiles parked just outside the back door, a large Polaris and a smaller Ski-Doo.

"Have you ever driven a motorcycle?" He zipped up his thermal jump suit.

"Lots."

"Good. The idea of leaning into curves is the same. Gas is on the right. Brakes are on the left. Ride with one finger on the brakes at all times but make sure you let off on the gas before hitting the brakes. This machine weighs more than 650 pounds so do not put a leg out. It will break off."

"Shifting pattern?"

"It's automatic."

"Rick. The head light is out on my Ski-Doo."

"We're just riding to the river and we'll make it back before sunset. I'll lead. Watch my tail light but also pay attention to my hand signals. If I raise my fist it means stop. If I wave it means slow down. If I pump my fist in the air it means let's go, baby." He climbed on his bigger snow mobile, started the engine, pulled down his goggles and pumped his fist, taking off slowly down the driveway.

We took a right turn onto his residential street and then crossed it onto a narrow path where trees had been harvested. It looked like a white street. Rick stopped and I pulled alongside him. "Steer clear of dark snow. That's a pond that hasn't frozen yet. Avoid bumps in the snow which might be tree trunks. You hit one of those and the bike will stop while you turn into superman, flying over the handlebars. It will also tear off the tracks." Then he pumped his fist and took off like a bat out of hell. Trying to catch him, I hit sixty miles an hour which made for a very cold wind chill factor. All of my winter gear kept me warm but I wore a scarf like a mask over my nose and mouth. My breath seeped out top and fogged my glasses. I finally had to lower it a bit. I watched Rick veer off to one side and followed suit. I passed a patch of dark snow. Later, I repeated this and passed a suspicious lump in the snow. At one point we both passed a moose with a majestic six-foot antler spread, standing on the edge of our white highway, in the tree line. It must have stood seven feet high from the shoulders down. We drove by at more than fifty miles an hour and luckily, it did not attack us. This was the mating season. We also saw huge ravens which the Native Alaskans considered mystical. One of the few birds that does not fly south for the winter, it often has a wing span of four to five feet. There was no sign of man: no telephone lines, no streets, no houses — just white and trees.

Rick barreled along, almost losing me. His machine had a top speed of over one hundred miles per hour while mine had a top speed of about eighty. My world-record motorcycle speed was eighty-five and I was close to it. Tears formed at the corners of my eyes under the glasses and froze on my cheeks.

Rick's tail light got bright red as he slowed, waving his arm. I pulled alongside of him. "There's a creek up ahead. Let's take it slow and scout it out." We crept up on a crevice that must have measured seven feet across at the top. Six feet below was a running creek. Rick continued slowly along the rim. "Here! We can jump it here. I'll go first. You have to gun it." He drove back about fifty yards before opening the engine and speeding over a slight hump in the snow and became airborne and flew across the creek. On the other side, his tail light went bright and he turned the vehicle to face me, pumping his fist in the air.

"Jesus, Christ," I muttered as I gunned the engine. My Ski-Doo flew.

On the other side, Rick pulled up his goggles. His mustache and chin whiskers had long hanging icicles from his breath. "Nice Job! We're close to the river now."

Within minutes our machines stood near the banks of Snake River fifteen miles southeast of Dillingham. It had not yet frozen and looked majestic. Rick drove near the water mixed with snow and leaned away from it, doing a full circle in the snow. I tried the same with a different result: the Ski-

Doo sunk two feet in the snow. Rick dismounted, walked over and jerked the machine out. Then mounted his own machine and took off. My machine lurched forward about fifty yards and go stuck again.

When Rick came back, his idea was to lay down next to my machine and lift one of the skis. The machine ran up one of his legs.

"Nothing broke, just a bruised ego," Rick shouted as he struggled.

I turned the skis a smidgen and remounted the rail.

"Try it again but with very little gas. The idea is that I'll pull my leg free." I tapped the gas and the snowmobile jerked forward a few inches while Rick pulled his leg free and rolled away. His leggings hadn't torn, There was no blood and he stood up and hobbled around. "I'll need a hot bath with Epsom salts tonight, Look at the sun!"

In the autumn the sun begins to race across the sky like a curve ball. We managed to get his machine away from the river and took off like banshees, heading back to Dillingham, racing the setting sun.

It was already dusk when I saw Rick's red tail light go up. He had already cleared the creek. For some reason, I hesitated, stopped. Took a deep breath and gunned the engine. We flew but did not clear it. The front skis lanced the other side's bank, the machine tilted towards my left and I fell, somehow landing on my feet in about two feet of water. Wet boots and leggings are not a good sign in sub-freezing temperatures. I looked up, the machine was literally in the air, suspended. I quickly walked downstream, afraid that it might fall on me.

With Rick's help and a rope, I climbed out. His machine was not strong enough to pull the smaller machine out. Just when we were glancing at the setting sun and discussing riding tandem on his machine. Another snow mobile pulled. The driver was wearing a pea cap and tinted goggles, like the lone ranger. He waved, got off his machine and hooked up another rope without a word. Rick mounted his. The Lone Ranger did a fist pump and the two pulled the Ski-Doo out. The Lone Ranger untied his rope, tucked it into a jacket pocket and waved as he drove off at top speed.

"Who was that?" I asked Rick.

"No idea. Let's get out of here. I'll go a bit slower. Follow about twenty yards behind me and pay attention to my tail light."

Luckily, there was no cloud cover and a fairly full moon which illuminated the snow. Janice had left the porch spotlight on to guide us up the driveway. We parked. Rick jumped off his machine and jogged back to mine as I tried to climb off but my feet weren't working well. I stumbled.

"I'm good."

"No, you're not." Rick put one of my arms around his neck and helped me towards the back door. My legs started to knot up and my hands shook uncontrollably. He opened the door and yelled. "Janice! Wool blanket now."

Janice appeared in the Arctic room and together they stripped me naked. Now I was really shaking. One of his daughters handed Janice a wool blanket which they wrapped me in and started to walk me back to the pool room. They sat me down on a chair. Another blanket appeared. Soon, Janice had a tiny tub of hot water to set my feet in. While Rick rubbed my hands, she massaged my calves and feet. I felt very strange.

Within minutes, there was a cup of hot chocolate as Rick stoked up a fire and they moved my chair closer. "Just relax and warm up," said Rick.

"I'll dry his clothes," said Janice.

That's how I dried my clothes on Christmas Eve.

Ross Alan Smith

The public works director, my former scout master, had been right: it was a very eccentric bunch housed in a strange building in the middle of nowhere and I liked it immediately. The property was not even accessed by a paved road which meant that I had to drive my moped extra slow to keep the back wheel from sliding. This had been a cattle ranch for many decades, a few miles north of Scottsdale's downtown. The ramshackle bunkhouse with ancient wooden framed windows, cracked siding with peeling paint was maybe 1,800 square feet, surrounded by fifteen-foot-high oleanders. There was no sign. Not even on the old wooden door.

The front door opened to a tiny ten by ten-foot walled alcove where a secretary sat at a desk, answering a telephone and typing at the same time. She motioned for me to sit down on a chair next to her desk while casually dressed people walked by one way and another. I soon found out that there were only two interior doors. One led to a tiny bathroom. Within minutes, a man about my stature with longish dark hair dressed in a Hawaiian style cotton shirt, casual khaki trousers came out to shake my hand.

"Lihosit. I've heard about you. You're in the right place. This is where we save the world. I'm Ross Smith. Let me introduce you to the team."

The office had been remodeled from one giant bunkhouse into a tiny kitchen and a room on each side of the entrance alcove. Ross led me through one side where a tiny hall had been created to block off the kitchen area but the partition had circles cut through it. There were desks on each side but no walls or doors. Two were set off with "L" shaped bookshelves that also held hanging plants. One woman who was working a doctorate in geography dressed as if she was about to go on safari. Next to her was another woman dressed like a real estate agent with a necklace and high heels. She had a master's degree in public administration and chain smoked brown wrapped cigarettes. There were two architectural students who worked as draftsmen dressed in blue jeans and sandals. One sported a long beard while the other had a droopy cowboy mustache. They were seated at drafting tables. The room had two tiny alcoves without doors: one for a senior draftsman and the other for the city architect. The city architect, Gerry Maskulka, had shoulder length brown hair. That day he wore a cowboy shirt, blue jeans and cowboy boots as he chained smoked thin cigars. The giant ashtray on his desk overflowed with butts. Next to it was an autographed photo of a television star from decades before, Rick Nelson. Some people hunched over drafting tables. Others sat with their shoes off and feet propped up as they read a report or book.

The other side of the building was very similar except it had a semicircular cowboy fireplace made of flagstone and a crackling fire with sweet smelling mesquite. There were no name plates, no inane chatter, no machines buzzing (but some mechanical type writers clacking), nobody running or yelling. It seemed like a cross between a public library and someone's living room.

There was also one single large room with four walls and a door, a conference room which we called the war room. Aside from the bathroom, this was the only interior door in the shop.

During break, someone might run down the tiny hall yelling through the cut circles in the wall, "Frisbee!" and there was an immediate clatter as people put on shoes or grabbed hats. Within seconds all seventeen of us were in the backyard, also screened by fifteen-foot-tall oleanders, laughing and running. Maybe someone might yell, "Wood cutting time!" and a large group assembled in back to cut our firewood. I'm sure this never happened in city hall. This was the youngest crew I ever worked with in my long career. The elder on staff was our director who was thirty-five. The draftsmen and I were the youngest at twenty-two.

Ross was the number two man in the office, the people person. With a crew that included artists, amateur archaeologists, hikers, kayakers, racquetball enthusiasts and

Frisbee nuts, Ross was more like a straw boss herding cats. He never yelled but he seemed to show up when there was a problem and always had a quiet solution or options that made sense.

Our job was to create Scottsdale, Arizona's new general plan in eight parts (called elements), guiding the city's growth between the years 1975 and 2000. We started with a population projection and vehicle estimates. This led to an idea of how wide roads would have to be or if new ones might be required. This led to ideas about land uses, economics and even environmental concerns. We generally operated like a gang of kids. For instance, there are several ways to project a population. Several of us tried. Once a week we met in the war room, a long narrow conference room with a table and walls covered by a thick pinboard material, so we could hang up maps, graphs and photos before we argued. When things got out of hand, Ross usually told a joke and calmed everyone down.

As the lowest of the low on the office totem pole, I did whatever was asked. I helped the secretary organize our files. I built a map rack and organized maps. I punched numbers on a calculator. After working in warehouses and paint shops I liked the idea that injuries in a planning office included paper cuts and staple punctures. I especially liked puffing on my corn cob pipe as I worked. Often the ladies remarked, "I like the scent of that tobacco."

One day as Ross passed my wobbly table next to the water cooler, he stopped. Colored pencils and markers were strewn all over. "See Lihosit? Everything you need to know about urban planning you learned in kindergarten."

We had no counter to meet the public because generally, we did not. That was for the downtown boys called current planning. Today it would be difficult to find a town of 63,000 inhabitants with seventeen people working in a long-range planning office.

Within months, my hair got scraggily. I grew my first caterpillar mustache and switched to sandals and Mexican cotton shirts. Ross poured himself a cup of coffee next to my desk. "I heard you're lookin' for a place closer to work." I nodded. "Come by my place tonight."

Ross, his wife Karen and their two daughters lived less than two miles from where I grew up. They were buying a half-acre with two Second World War tin roofed clapboard houses thrown together to form a duplex across the street from an old crabby lady who lived in a ranch style home adjoining a riding stable. Like the bunkhouse, Ross's place was rustic, very rustic. The part he offered me was a two-room efficiency. It had one large entrance room that served as a kitchen-living room and a doored tiny bedroom with bath. This was cooled by an evaporative cooler that Ross had placed on the roof. Karen had built the raised wooden entrance patio out of discarded railroad ties. She had also constructed a small patio at their own back door with discarded oven baked brick. The yard had no vegetation at all. It was the original desert landscape with occasional tufts of weeds. In back, there was a collection of old school buses in the process of being turned into living quarters on wheels (recreational vehicles), an old British MG that rarely ran and layers of old airplane parts since the original owner had operated some kind of airplane repair service. Once in a blue moon, Ross got the old MG running and drove his daughters round the yard, like an amusement park ride. They smiled and laughed.

Ross and Karen had no objection to me painting the inside. He also let me rummage around the yard for old parts. I found a weathered old board and mounted pieces of machinery spray painted black. At a local hardware store, I bought colored rubber bands which I placed on my steel montage as if they were belts. The result was a wall mounted conversation piece. Ross's only comment was, "It can be removed, right?"

A friend with a pick-up helped me to steal a large wooden spool which had been used to hold electrical cable. This served as a table. Yard sales supplied me with an old giant floor fan, a beat-up bed, two stools, a bamboo set of easy chairs, a metal folding chair, a tiny lamp table and a very old cactus lamp. *Voila!* I had a very crazy looking bachelor pad.

Karen did not agree. "If I were single and you brought me here, I'd run as fast as I could!" Occasionally we drank beer outside on folding chairs, watching the sun set on an orange and crimson Arizona sky. If Ross needed help holding a wire or whatever, he came and banged on my door. With a meager salary, no television or telephone, I was always home reading a book.

At work, we made steady progress, finally making a presentation to the city council and planning commission who made some suggestions. The war room walls were now filled with colored maps, aerial photos, charts and graphs. Collectively, we called these the "zoomies." It was all just progressing but off on the horizon, a storm had been moving our way. The sky to the south turned brown and it moved faster and faster towards us. The federal government had supported Israel in a 1973 war. In retribution, Middle Eastern oil rich countries stopped selling to us. Gasoline stations had lines of cars, sometimes a quarter mile long. Fist fights broke out at the pumps.

My moped got 483 miles per gallon. I used about one quarter of a gallon each week. After buying a metal can at the hardware store, I drove up past the line where people swore, bickered and fought, holding up my empty can and yelling, "I only need one gallon for my lawn mower." They always smiled and waved me through. But the city where I worked was a different matter. Scottsdale was a tourist spot. Midwesterners drove up during the winter months, traded in their rust buckets for new cars and drove home as it warmed. The city depended upon that sales tax. With the oil embargo, tourism evaporated. The city had an economic crisis. Worse yet, construction slowed as the nation entered an economic recession. No building? No need for builders. I soon learned that under such circumstances, government agencies always begin with lay-offs in the library, the recreation and planning departments.

On a Monday morning, we had a meeting in the war room. The director explained, "You're here because we believe in you and your work. These are hard times and the city fathers have decided to lay-off employees but this is no reflection on you and your work. I will be speaking individually to each of you whose last day will be Friday."

More than half of us got talked to, including me. The job was not set up to make us rich. We all wanted to save the world and felt as if the world had just kicked us in the teeth. We felt worthless. Just like always, Ross appeared at my table. "Talk to Maskulka."

The city architect had made some calls and found out that a local planning firm needed help with a general plan for a neighboring community. That same night, three of us formed a partnership and began a proposal which was accepted in less than a week. We were no longer public employees but business owners. It all happened so fast.

Time went by quickly as we completed our tasks and moved on. Each of us went in a different direction and I was unemployed again. That's when Ross banged on my door. "The engineering department has a temporary position with benefits. It won't last long. Go down to personnel."

So, I worked at a temporary job for the City of Scottsdale until the Peace Corps called me to make me an offer. So where to store some belongings for two years? It wasn't much: a few boxes with old clothing and kitchen utensils. Ross stacked the boxes in his outside storage closet.

We kept in touch. Some thirty-six years later when both my sons were attending Northern Arizona University in Flagstaff, Ross called. "Karen and I own a split-level summer home on the south side of campus. We don't use it much and wanted to rent it out to college kids. Do you think Zeke and Anson might be interested in managing it? They could live there for a discounted rate." Ross put a roof over two generations' heads and opened the war room door for a career in saving the world.

Armando Votto Paz

Armando Votto Paz wasn't just any Community Development foreman. He not only got us what we needed but stood by us whistling away the dark clouds. I didn't want to let him down but being young, my genes were jumping. I was in love and had just slunk back from a clandestine trip to Mexico City.

Secrets (like a Mexican girlfriend) are easier heard than kept. I feared the worst when Armando surprised me at my La Ceiba office where I was typing legends for my own maps. He paged through my report's appendix, checking calculations and smiled before suggesting that I take the day off. He had to visit another volunteer in an isolated village. Since I had never been to the place and he could use some company, he thought it a good fit. We climbed aboard his brand new imported North American four-wheel drive vehicle. The sunlight, reflecting from the dashboard, made me shield my eyes.

Within thirty minutes, he had crossed the one-lane wide bridge constructed of railroad ties over the Rio Cangrejal. He drove almost due east, bumping along a dirt rut which wound through jungle only a quarter mile from an invisible ocean shrouded by a green mass. Parrots chattered but if you listened attentively, you could hear waves lapping the shore, somewhere to our left. Gone were the sounds of railroad engines, bells, clinking as a train engineer backed down the wooden dock pushing boxcars full of green bananas to be loaded into German or Japanese or British or Chinese or North American freighters only two blocks from my office; gone was the white, blinding sunlight illuminating silhouettes of men stripped to the waist as they furiously worked aluminum conveyor belts; gone was the salt brine suspended in air that stuck to our sweaty backs. Huge bright green and orange jungle parrots squawked loud as Armando's jeep slowed to cross a stream which had washed out our rut. A break in the canopy above permitted a single ray of white light to shine down, reflecting off the clear running water that gurgled as a bead of salty perspiration dropped off my mustache onto my lips. Only a few miles from the third most populated city in the nation and there was no visible sign of man except for a lone orange colored rut, sliced by streams.

Armando whistled, hung one crooked arm out of his open window, steering with the other as we plowed through the stream. The jeep fishtailed while he pumped the accelerator and laughed. A shower of water flew up past our side windows like geysers. Then we stopped dead. The parrots squawked louder.

We were stuck. Trucks did not pass often, sometimes for days. We took off our shirts, rolled up our pants and waded out. We gathered vines as close to the water's edge as possible since Honduras had pit vipers, tropical rattlesnakes, fer-de-lance, coral snakes and even bushmasters. Within forty minutes we had created some fair ramps and Armando whooped as the jeep lurched forward and through the stream.

Armando laughed and pulled the jeep up onto solid ground as I splashed in the water like a crazy man. My brain was verb-conjugated fried by that report in Spanish. I suspected that Armando must have felt the same after months of sitting stiffly behind a desk in the capital city, wearing a tie and repeating "Yes," to his boss. He got out of the jeep and joined me in the stream. Soon, we rolled and played in the water, laughing hysterically while parrots squawked.

Armando was a fine guide. Later, after an hour following close to the ocean, he stopped in front of a shack built of discarded lumber, rough hewn logs and metal alongside a bridged creek where white water rushed over boulders. A toothless old woman dressed in greasy rags sold us two warm soft drinks and some saltine crackers. Armando opened the bottle with his teeth just before we reboarded the jeep. We drank and ate as he drove.

A tall black Carib who wore only trousers and carried a rifle stepped in front of our jeep. Armando stopped and quickly told me that this was the watchman. Just up ahead, the ocean's waves crashed. The underbrush thinned and on both sides of this dirt rut, palm trees towered. As the man stepped up to Armando's window, Armando told me in English that this had once been a foreign owned plantation for the export of coconuts. Although still foreign-owned, it had been abandoned when the price dropped.

Armando told the man in Spanish that we were sent by so and so because we were scientists who had just discovered that coconut was a cure for cancer. In no time, said Armando, the foreign company would reopen and there would be jobs for everyone. The man smiled and ran ahead. He climbed a tree and brought down coconuts for us. Overhead, dry palm fronds crackled. The rhythmic waves broke. After a quick swim in the ocean, a refreshing drink of raw coconut milk and a meal of its white meat dug out with homemade coconut skin spoons, we drove off. The man waved his rifle in the air while smiling broadly.

Armando took a fork in the road that led up a mountain. We left the sound and smell of the ocean behind and they were replaced with bushes and thistles scraping across the jeep's body and birds taking to wing. My back itched from the dried ocean salt which clung to my back in white strips. Armando drove into a tiny hidden valley where corn stalks choked the narrow rut.

He parked in front of a low ranch style adobe building with a corrugated tin roof. He slipped on his soiled white shirt, combed his hair straight back while looking in his muddy side-view mirror, explaining that it was wise to look like authority. What's-his-face (a pseudonym), the volunteer we were here to visit, had problems. Armando put on his dark glasses before his door creaked open and a mist of dust floated in.

"Stay here."

Within minutes, Armando climbed back in alone and jammed the transmission into reverse, crunching gears. "He's not at work again."

Armando drove two miles out of town to a lone tiny adobe home. Its metal roof reflected waves of heat. Inside, what's-his-face lounged on a living room hammock. At first, he was friendly, only occasionally wiping his dark hair from his brow in a peculiar habit. When Armando asked a few questions about work, what's-his-face began to pace while he wiped at his hair faster, even when it was not on his brow. His voice rose to a squeal. He told stories about a string of failures and had reason for each. Armando listened and told all the same stories over with a different twist. The volunteer paced faster still.

Armando unloaded some supplies from his jeep a left a handbill about our upcoming group excursion across the country to the island of Ampala on the Pacific coast. He told what's-his-face that he could charge his travel expenses to the Peace Corps as a per diem.

"I expect to see you," Armando told him in English. We climbed back into the jeep. "He needs a vacation," said Armando while turning the ignition key.

For the next two hours the jeep's engine whined. We were bucked up and down, side to side, as Armando veered past chuckholes. He maneuvered angles and forded streams without stopping until we neared the railroad tie bridge on the outskirts of La Ceiba. We waited as a large group of black women dressed in turbans and simple long pieces of cotton cloth wrapped around their bodies, walked across while carrying bundles on their heads. Without the jungle canopy it was much hotter. Armando unbuttoned the top three buttons of his shirt, took off his dark glasses and ran a hand through his hair. He slumped back into the seat and quizzed me about my Mexican girlfriend. He knew her name but never mentioned my secret vacation.

"My cousin married a Mexican girl," he said as he thumped his palm on the steering wheel. "They have a saying in Mexico: you marry the bride's entire family." Armando looked at me smirking, "Watch out *gringo*."

Rich Yurman

Young junior college students filed out of class as our instructor took his baseball jacket off of the back of a chair and slipped it on. I closed my notebook. Rich Yurman pushed back his bushy red, streaked with grey hair with both hands and put on his baseball cap.

I walked towards his desk. "Would you mind if I wrote short stories instead of poems?"

"Have you ever written a poem?"

"Not since grade school."

"I've noticed that you're older than the rest so you must have had some interesting experiences. Why not write at least one poem?" Yurman was famous on campus: a PhD from the Massachusetts Institute of Technology in math and literature, published poet and playwright as well as the editor of the poetry magazine.

So, I wrote the poem. "It has promise," he told me afterwards but I repeated my plea. He adjusted his cap to one side, jauntily. "The poem whispers that there is more to tell. Maybe that could be a short story – just don't mention this to the rest of our class. You'll still have to complete the same number of assignments."

This was what my wife and I refer to as the beginning of our Bohemian Years: she studying something besides science and I sharpening my writing skills. Community colleges in California had been free until Ronald Reagan, who considered all public colleges and universities "a haven for communist sympathizers…..," changed that (I had heard the same phrase in Honduras during a military regime). I paid fifteen dollars for Rich's course. Rich was my very first published mentor. I wrote and wrote and rewrote. Rich did not line edit. He was also the first to always wear a baseball cap.

"We can always get someone to fix spelling and grammar is spongy, like a nerf ball. Try reviewing the use of commas in the Chicago Manual of Style. It's eleven pages long and in the end, the conclusion is 'Do what you feel.'" I continued to write. Rich always noted questions on my efforts like, "Why? Who is this? Give me details. Could this be said in less words?" Likewise, class was different. He never noted a grade. Once I asked him about that.

"I thought you were here to improve. Hand me that paper." He wrote a big "A" across the page. "Does it matter?" He shrugged his shoulders.

Rich brought in other poets to recite for us, many times about political topics. There were a lot. The Reagan Administration purposefully created a recession to wring out inflation. The local result was 50,000 homeless in the Bay Area. Three blocks from the tourist stop for the famous cable cars, homeless had pitched tents on city sidewalks. Beggars were everywhere. The City Planning Director lost use of one of his legs when a homeless person whacked him across the kneecap with a crow bar in broad day-light. Thousands of young, healthy gay men developed bruises and were dead within seventy-two hours. The nameless disease bred paranoia. It turned into a national plague before the federal government began to investigate. Mayor Feinstein met with big spenders to continue Home Port status for the USS Missouri battleship while hundreds of protestors waved signs and screamed outside. Internationally, the same administration started a counter-revolution in Nicaragua funded by the sale of drugs and sent arms to a government in El Salvador as a measure to forestall civil strife there. Even national celebrities called Central America our next Vietnam. Rich invited speakers, many of whom passed out flyers about the next protest march. Local newspapers sometimes showed Rich leading such protests.

We were also invited to outside poetry readings. Instead of piling more books on our reading list, he suggested we meet authors, listen to lectures. "Good writing begins with good listening," he said.

He also recommended that we watch the San Francisco Mime Group perform in Golden Gate Park. One Sunday my wife and I rode buses downtown. We wandered until finding two hundred people on blankets, in front of a puppet show. It was a Punch and Judy puppet show about the American defense budget. When the tiny curtain closed. A man dressed in lavish women's clothing walked up and began to berate the puppets, then the audience. Immediately, her many servants whisked off the puppet show box and we were caught in the middle of a short skit, a farce, about Ferdinand and Imelda Marcos, the first couple in the Philippines. This was followed by men dressed as nuns, called the Sisters of Perpetual Indulgence, who had a comedy routine about gender. The skits lasted about forty minutes and when completed the troupe took a bow, broke down their tiny stage and walked in different directions. This was very different from the nightly news during the Reagan Administration. Very different and Rich was an instigator who wore a baseball cap.

Who is this guy? I found a few of his poems, published in an underground poetry magazine sold at City Lights. A few years later it would be included in a tome called *A Perfect Pair: He Whispered, She Shouted* about his Central European immigrant grandparents who basically raised him. His love for them was mixed with a wonderful sense of humor. In "The Daily Forward," Rich explained "She'd talk to him about the articles in a fast paced, clipped language I could barely understand even when her teeth were in." Much of his poetry was a narrative without rhyming but a definite rhythm. There was no introspective navel contemplation, no shaking a fist at the sky. So, where did the cap come from?

Skyline College hosted an annual poetry conference. Rich, the master of ceremonies, was dressed the same in baggy khakis, a plain cotton button-down shirt open at the neck and high-top, canvas tennis shoes. His voice was soft and gentle.

One of the participants was Katherine Harer, a former student who he now considered his equal. She read the poem title "Nothing" which began "Poets are always writing about nothing." This was applauded.

When she finished, someone in the audience shouted, "Read, Rich!" Katherine handed Rich a thick folder full of typed pages. "You want something green? Eat a pickle…" he began as if he were a native-born Yiddish speaker trying English. It was a poem about his father. Years later, this would be included in his book *Giraffe*. Smiles filled the room.

The crowd called for more but Rich explained, "I've got a softball game and we're in the playoffs!" He reached into his back pocket, pulled out his cap and waved.

I managed to write a poem and ten short stories for Rich over fifteen weeks. They were much better than my first novel which should have been titled *crapola*. My writing life led me to other classes but none as exciting as Richs'. He retired at fifty-five after thirty-two years of teaching. A hall filled with students, former students and staff to wish him good luck.

A few years later, after our Bohemian Era ended, he called. "Have you been writing?"

"Do you want to see?"

"*Nudnik*! What's doin' there?"

He traded an autographed copy of *The Perfect Pair* for one of my humorous travel books. Telephone calls are clipped like telegrams, so we became pen pals as my wife, two sons and I now lived one hundred fifty miles southeast of San Francisco. From that moment on, Rich became my *de facto* ideas man. All of his comments were noted on a matrix along with those from another friend. Usually, I sent them both a second or third draft to mull over. My wife and I visited him in Oakland where he pulled out his wallet to show us photos of the children he had agreed to tutor for free. On another solo trip, I met and played with his infant grandson who ambled around the kitchen floor, smiling as we toasted lemonade. Rich had taken on his grandfather Abe's role.

Retrieving mail became an exciting short walk. I was always searching for the envelope that had Rich's name crossed off and mine written next to it. He reused envelopes. Our correspondence was like candy. He sent me new published poetry and I sent him my new work. The letters always started with comments about that trade, a few personal details and then, current events. Unlike most, Rich did not just consult the television news about current events, but magazines and books as well. It was a great intellectual badminton game of exchanging opinions.

My elder son, Zeke, was a member of his high school academic decathlon team and that year, a portion of their studies included poetry. I called Rich.

"Who are they reading? *Oy vey*, that's good. Has he ever heard poetry read? Drive him up. We'll fix that."

The entire family drove to the border of Oakland and Berkeley where Rich and Claudine had been living for many years. The Victorian home had three levels and was built on a hill so that you entered street-side in the middle: bedrooms upstairs, more rooms downstairs with an exit to the backyard and a living room and kitchen in the middle. The front yard was a mass of huge shrubs which I had to hold back so the family could pass. The front door bell was broken so I clanged their metal-on-metal knocker.

"This looks like a scary movie," said Anson, my younger son. Inside, Rich seated us in the crowded and dark living room. We were surrounded by antique clocks and music boxes of all sizes and shapes. Their clicking sounded like a chorus of crickets. Even the table held a menagerie of music boxes.

Claudine came out, dressed in a grandma's printed robe, her hair in curlers, carrying a silver tray with a pitcher and glasses. "I'm getting ready for the opening of my play tonight but I made some lemonade. I have tickets for you."

"Open the curtains, Rich, so they can see." She pulled a drawer, grabbed some clinking antique metal keys and said, "Let me show you my collection," walking around her table where the largest music box of all sat: a giant metal carousel with horses and riders. Claudine fiddled until she found the right key and cranked it. Music started, the carousel went around, the horses moved up and down while their riders turned their heads from side to side. Next, she pulled a small box from a shelf and explained that it was her oldest. From her ring of keys, she found the right one and inserted it into the box. Beautiful chimes played. Simultaneously, dozens of clocks began to chime the hour.

Claudine moved to one wall. "This is a player piano from the nineteenth century. It works on these spools," she held one up, then inserted a key. It played "On a Bicycle Built for Two." The clocks chimed the quarter hour. Claudine gave us a history lesson on the player piano. When the clocks chimed the half hour, she looked startled. "Oh! I have to get ready. I hope to see you at the play."

"Are you guys hungry?" asked Rich. My boys nodded. "Let's take a walk to my favorite restaurant."

Even though Rich carried a cane, he walked as if he were a mountain climber, with a long gait. Soon, the boys, Maggie-Rita and Rich left me in the dust. Every so often, they stopped, and waited for me to catch up, puffing on a cigarette. "Those are bad for you," said Rich.

"You're right. I'll quit, *mañana.*"

Rich held the door of a storefront restaurant with all kinds of colors painted on the trim and the old wooden window frames. Inside, African paintings were hung on brightly colored walls. The waitresses were clothed in traditional Ethiopian long unbleached cotton dresses with embroidery around the neck, sleeves and hemline. There was a long line of people waiting inside but Rich had a reservation.

"This place is popular," he said.

Luckily, the menus had photos of the food. "No matter what we order," explained Rich, "they will serve it all on one huge platter, covered on the bottom by flatbread made of an African grain. It looks like a skinny tan tortilla. They call it *injera.*" There was a lively discussion with the waitress about the food. When the platter was set down on the middle of our table, it looked like the walls: a mixture of all primary colors in small bowls. Rich showed us how to rip off a small piece of flatbread and pinch food and eat it without forks or knives, like Mexicans do with *tortillas.*

After the late lunch, we walked some more to a store front café, bustling with an eclectic crowd. Old fogies with white hair pulled back into pony tails and other oldsters with shaved heads talked to each other. Youngsters with orange, green and purple hair joined some of the conversations. One guy had his head shaved except for one strip down the center (a Mohawk). The center was about eighteen inches long, glued to stand straight up and painted purple. Men and women wore nose rings, lip rings, ear rings and probably others out of sight. There were tattoos of birds, dragons and even military tattoos with insignias and numbers. People wore shoes, boots and sandals. We all looked a bit like Central Valley yahoos but Zeke, dressed in his athletic letterman's jacket, might have stood out more. Patrons could care less. The crowd was smiling and dozens of conversations went on, creating a buzz. Chairs rattled as they were moved, hard nailed boots clicked, the coffee machines hissed and waiters dressed in white aprons yelled.

"Two café lattes for Guillermo!"

"Coffee cake a la mode for Suzie Cream Cheese."

"Regular coffee for Jack Meoff."

We all chose a drink and Anson ran into an adjoining room to get us a table. The place was filling quickly in anticipation of Open Mic Night with poetry readings. Rich and Zeke, carrying his black academic decathlon three ring binder, walked behind.

"So, tell me about this competition, Zeke," said Rich.

Maggie-Rita and I found the three of them in deep conversation. We motioned to Anson and slipped away to study the art on every wall while Rich and Zeke talked. Finally, with standing room only, a microphone and podium decorated with rainbows were set up. A lady with short spiked hair introduced Rich who read a poem and the open mic began. Some of the speakers were very experienced while others seemed nervous. After about an hour, Rich pointed to his wrist and we quickly and silently walked to the door to begin our hike to Rich's house, uphill. The four of them had an animated conversation as I struggled behind.

In front of Rich and Claudine's house, we piled into our car and followed Rich's directions to a grocery store where Rich bought a bouquet, then on to a community theater near San Ramon, a few miles away. "It's opening night," explained Rich to the boys. "You're supposed to give the actors flowers."

The play was titled "The Oldest Profession" and it was not Eugene O'Neill, but rather a comedy. Five minutes into the play, Anson leaned over to ask me, "Where's Claudine?"

"She's the lead," I whispered. While she looked, walked and talked like a grandma at home, on stage she acted like a woman twenty-five years younger, full of energy and in skimpy outfits, very curvaceous.

Anson nudged Zeke, "That's Claudine!" Zeke's eyes got big.

Rich was now publishing more than in his entire life. I arranged a poetry reading and book sale at the only book store in Madera, a small farming community. It was a different audience of plain-dressed and plain-spoken who bought a few copies of his latest poetry tome.

Later, we drove to Zeke's high school for a baseball game. As we walked towards the bleachers, Rich pulled his favorite baseball cap from his back pocket. With both hands, he pushed back white wisps of hair before placing the cap. "I had to give up softball two years ago at the age of sixty-five."

"Why?"

"I hurt my hip sliding into second base." He smiled broadly.

Bibliographic Note

Fernando Bastida Monterrubio A slightly different version of this piece can be found in *Jesus Was Arrested in Mexico City and Missed the Wedding*, Lawrence F. Lihosit, N. Charleston, SC, CreateSpace, 2017.

Rafael Iglesias Bermudez A more detailed description of the Case of Santa Anita is contained in the book titled *Years On and Other Travel Essays*, Lawrence F. Lihosit, Bloomington, IN, iUniverse, 2011. See "Roads and Light Rail."

Mario Ribera Arteaga is an excerpt from *Travels in South America*, Lawrence F. Lihosit, N. Charleston, SC, CreateSpace, 2017.

Herb Schmidt also appears in the book titled *Years On and Other Travel Essays*, Lawrence F. Lihosit, Bloomington, IN, iUniverse, 2011. See "Champion Sprinter."

Gloria Jean Link, Rick Shilanski & Dallas Nelson for more about Dillingham, see *Years On and Other Travel Essays*, Lawrence F. Lihosit, Bloomington, IN, iUniverse, 2011, "Bush Alaska."

Acknowledgements

The cover photo was provided by Dra. L. Margarita Solis Kitsu de Lihosit. Marissa Ruiz formatted the cover. My good buddy Will James edited this book. Like old-school newspapermen, we recruited all-star readers to check for typographical errors. Copy editors included; Steve Cannon, Sandy Elliott, Bob Forster, Anson K. Lihosit, Ezequiel K. Lihosit, Bob Petit, Dra. L. Margarita Solis Kitsu de Lihosit and Bryant Wieneke.

About the Author

Lawrence F. Lihosit was born in the southern suburbs of Chicago, Illinois in 1951. His family later moved to Arizona where he graduated from grade school, high school and Arizona State University. He reluctantly served in the U.S. Army Reserves during the closing years of the Vietnam War and enthusiastically volunteered for the Peace Corps (Honduras, 1975-1977). His travels and work have taken him from the salmon spawning Nushagak River Basin in southwestern Alaska to the fertile Argentine Pampas. His continuing studies have included master's coursework in urban planning at *la Universidad Nacional Autónoma de México* in Mexico City, art and creative writing at Skyline College in San Bruno, California and education at California State University Fresno. Now retired, he earned his living as an urban planner for many years, working in Honduras, Mexico, Alaska, Arizona and California. His literary work has garnered positive reviews and attention. *South of the Frontera: A Peace Corps Memoir* received a U.S. Congressional commendation (2010) while *Years On and Other Travel Essays* was awarded Best Travel Book (2012) by Peace Corps Writers. The author of nineteen books, he and his wife raised two sons in Madera where they have lived since 1995, volunteering along the way. Mr. Lihosit served as an officer in his union (*Madera County Mid-Management*) for seven years and coached youth soccer, baseball and basketball.

Other Books by the Author

South of the Frontera; A Peace Corps Memoir

Peace Corps Bibliography

Peace Corps Chronology; 1961-2010

Peace Corps Experience: Write and Publish Your Memoir

Slacker's Confession: Essays and Sketches

Madera Sketchbook

Neighbors: Oral History from Madera, California (V 1,2 3)

Back to School and Other Poems

Border Penance and Other Stories

Those Who Are Gone (A Novel)

Americruise

*Jesus Was Arrested in Mexico City
and Missed the Wedding*

Travels in South America

Across the Yucatan

Made in the USA
Las Vegas, NV
28 July 2023

75371151R00090